Feedback on *Advice for a Successful Career in the Accounting Profession*

"By leveraging Jerry's advice and knowledge, I have every reason to believe you can have a successful career. I wish this book were available when I was starting my career—read it now and you'll have an advantage over me and others that come after you."

— *From the introduction by Ernie Almonte, former Chairman of the AICPA*

"I have worked closely with Jerry on the board of Faith in the Future, which is focused on preserving and strengthening Catholic education in the Philadelphia region. He brought the same energy and passion to writing this book as he does to our mission. Accounting students and early-career professionals will benefit from his advice."

— *Ed Hanway, Board Chair of Faith in the Future Foundation and former CEO of CIGNA Corp.*

"The Maginnis book should be required reading, not just for future accountants but for all business majors. His tactical breakdown of the elements that key success is both comprehensive and concise. It is well written and Maginnis connects the academic to the practical with a unique and persuasive approach. This book is for those studying for the field, just entering, or even for practitioners a little further along in their careers. Highly recommend this read!"

— *Tom Foley, President, The Association of Independent Colleges and Universities of Pennsylvania*

"As a college student, I felt the book was very relatable and that it provided a lot of helpful and insightful advice. It is a great book for students who are thinking about majoring in accounting, students already studying accounting and young professionals beginning their career in accounting."

— *Brianna Vechesky, candidate for a Master of Accounting with Data Analytics, Villanova University*

"Jerry has written a guide that should be in the hands of every first-year college business student. Drawing on his long career in accounting and his wealth of experience he provides a roadmap for students to chart their path to career success. Making smart choices as students start their college experience can lead to tremendous advantages when students enter the world of work. Our students will receive this manual during their 'Orientation' to the Haub School of Business."

— *Joseph A. DiAngelo, Jr., EdD, Dean, Erivan Haub School of Business, Saint Joseph's University, Past Chair, Association to Advance Collegiate Schools of Business (AACSB)*

"*Advice for a Successful Career in the Accounting Profession* is a must read for students and young professionals that wish to learn more about the opportunities available in the accounting profession. The book does an outstanding job of covering the benefits available as well as what it will take to achieve success. Jerry Maginnis has decades of experience in the profession and has written a book that is easy to read and understand!"

— *Frank Ross, CPA, Director of the Center for Accounting Education at Howard University*

"While these leadership lessons are especially relevant for those pursuing a career in professional services, particularly accounting, they are easily applicable to anyone embarking on any career, as well as great advice for life in general. Jerry has provided a sound roadmap to guide readers on a path that will help ensure a seamless transition into, and journey along, a successful and fulfilling career".

— *Mike Colgan, CEO, Pennsylvania Institute of Certified Public Accountants*

"In this book, Jerry shares practical insights useful to students and professionals of all ages who are interested in accounting. I encourage anyone who is seeking a fulfilling and successful career in either public accounting or business to read this book!"

— *Nathan Vrabel, Saint Joseph's University, B.S. in Accounting, May 2020*

"Straightforward, articulate and illuminating, this terrific book by Jerry Maginnis provides a transparent and informative overview of all aspects of the accounting profession. He highlights the many opportunities and rewards of an accounting career but also acknowledges the work required and challenges that will be experienced by successful professionals. Undergraduate business schools should make this book required reading for any students considering a career in accounting. The insights and personal experiences that Jerry shares from his many years in the profession include kernels of wisdom that will be valuable for accounting professionals at any point in their career."

— *Larry McAlee, Chief Financial Officer, Essent Group Ltd.*

Advice for a Successful Career in the Accounting Profession

How to Make Your Assets ^Exceed Your Liabilities

Greatly

By Jerry Maginnis, CPA

*Achieving Your Full Potential and Optimizing
the Benefits of Your Accounting Degree*

Published by John Wiley & Sons, Inc., Hoboken, New Jersey.
Published simultaneously in Canada.

For general information on our other products and services or for technical support, please contact our Customer Care Department within the United States at (800) 762-2974, outside the United States at (317) 572-3993 or fax (317) 572-4002.

Wiley also publishes its books in a variety of electronic formats. Some content that appears in print may not be available in electronic formats. For more information about Wiley products, visit our web site at www.wiley.com.

Library of Congress Cataloging-in-Publication Data:

Names: Maginnis, Jerry, author.
Title: Advice for a successful career in the accounting profession : how to make your assets greatly exceed your liabilities / by Jerry Maginnis, CPA.
Description: Hoboken, NJ : Wiley, 2021. | Includes index.
Identifiers: LCCN 2021038150 (print) | LCCN 2021038151 (ebook) | ISBN 9781119855286 (hardback) | ISBN 9781119855309 (adobe pdf) | ISBN 9781119855293 (epub)
Subjects: LCSH: Accounting. | Accountants. | Vocational guidance.
Classification: LCC HF5636 .M354 2021 (print) | LCC HF5636 (ebook) | DDC 657—dc23
LC record available at https://lccn.loc.gov/2021038150
LC ebook record available at https://lccn.loc.gov/2021038151

Cover Design and Illustrations: Rob Cuff
Author Photo: courtesy of the Author

SKY10034744_062022

Dedication

To my family: My brother, Tom, and sister, Jean; my brother, Kevin, and his wife, Barbara; my kids, Julie, Nikki, and Jerry, and their spouses/significant others, Sean, Tim, and Deanna; and my grandkids: Brayden, Gracie, Nick, Reese, Lukey, Sophie, Cameron, and Jake. You all are terrific, and I very much appreciate your love, encouragement, and support. But, most of all, to my wife and best friend, Lee Ann. You are the best!

The Maginnis family on the beach in Ocean City, New Jersey, Summer of 2020.

From left to right:
Top row: *Son in Law, Sean Geary, Daughter Julie, the Author and his wife, Lee Ann, son, Jerry, Daughter Nikki, and Son in Law, Tim Sickler.*

Bottom row: *Grandkids Brayden, Sophie, Gracie, Reese, Lukey, and Nick.*

Contents

Section Three—Building on Your Success as Your Career Advances

Introduction

With great trust and confidence, I recommend this book to any aspiring or current CPA.

Jerry Maginnis and I first met while serving on the Foundation Board of the American Institute of Certified Public Accountants. I quickly found Jerry to be a reliably smart, strategic thinker with a passion for getting things right, a truly thoughtful and personable team player with impeccable manners and adept communication skills. To this day, I continue to learn something new in every interaction with Jerry. He has a proven track record of excellence and an unwavering dedication to integrity.

Jerry's insights into the skills and opportunities of our profession are second to none. This book gives you an opportunity to have a person of character, competence, and class as your mentor. I only wish I had met Jerry earlier in my career so I could have benefited from his mentorship. I'm grateful now, though, to have his advice and counsel at this stage of my career and I encourage you to use this book as if he were sitting next to you answering your questions.

Our profession offers a wealth of specializations and niche practices— it's like a choose-your-own-adventure book; fully customizable and filled with opportunity if only you know where to look. Jerry's work will serve as a great reference book and roadmap to help you navigate the many corners and opportunities of accounting. Think of it as your guidebook and you'll find it takes you to places you couldn't have imagined.

This book is a valuable resource regardless of where you are in your professional journey. For the high school or college student who's just starting out, this book will introduce you to the profession, and help you identify opportunities, choose a path, and make critical early-stage decisions that will set you up for long-term success. For those early in their career, it will help you build the strong foundation that you'll need to be successful. And if you're a bit further along in your career, Jerry's advice and counsel will help you refine your capabilities, up-skill, re-skill, identify new opportunities, and find ways to give back.

By leveraging Jerry's advice and knowledge, I have every reason to believe you can have a successful career. I wish this book were available when I was starting my career—read it now and you'll have an advantage over me and others that come after you.

As someone who has benefited tremendously from a career as a CPA and strongly believes in the benefits and values of our profession, I can think of no one better than Jerry to guide you and advocate for our profession. Read his words, utilize his knowledge and benefit from the guidance of a tremendous CPA.

Enjoy your journey and I wish you a great and successful career.

Ernie Almonte CPA CGMA CFF
Former Chairman, American Institute of Certified Public Accountants
Former President, Association of Government Accountants

May 18, 2021

Why I Wrote This Book
(And How to Get the Most Out of It)

There are thousands of accounting books in circulation and more get written each year. Most are technical in nature. Textbooks used by college and university students discuss accounting theory and teach the "debits and credits." Professional literature, such as that published by the Financial Accounting Standards Board (FASB) or Public Company Accounting Oversight Board (PCAOB) detail the accounting and auditing standards. The Internal Revenue Code and related interpretations and regulations describe tax rules. Consultants and advisors offer insights on emerging business trends. Academics publish their research and practitioners write articles sharing their experience.

Given this vast body of knowledge, did we really need one more accounting book?

I concluded the answer to that question was yes. During my time as Executive in Residence at Rowan University, I've met dozens of accounting students who have many questions about the profession they are planning to enter. And, while working at KPMG, I met hundreds of early-career professionals eager for advice and suggestions on how to achieve a successful accounting career.

This book was written principally for those two groups. I hope that students majoring in accounting and professionals in the early stages of their careers will benefit. While people embark on their academic and professional careers at a variety of ages, many of the people this book aims to help will be between the ages of 18 and 28. I hope the book will also be helpful to others further along in their careers.

Before starting this project, I did some research to see whether a book like this had been written. I found some books by accountants that were essentially "memoirs." While there was some advice sprinkled throughout these books, they did not appear to be written primarily to offer advice. Similarly, there are books that explore accounting career paths and options, but they don't include a lot of practical advice on achieving success.

This book is an attempt to fill that void. I have tried to write down in one place, in a logical way and format, lessons I learned during my career and the related advice that I have offered many university students and early-career professionals in response to their "real-world" questions. While there were multiple dimensions in those questions, they had a common theme: How can I be successful in this profession? My answers to those questions are contained in this book and are based on my practical experience.

How to Get the Most Out of the Book

I've organized the book into three sections. The first six chapters contain advice aimed at college and university students. The next nine chapters focus on early-career professionals (those in the first five or six years of their careers, a critical time to form good habits). The final three chapters contain advice that I believe can benefit accountants of all ages.

Notwithstanding the target audience I've described, I would like to think that accountants a bit further along in their careers might also benefit from this book. Perhaps it will serve as a good refresher or reminder of concepts or principles that are important to their ongoing success.

So, maybe in an ideal world, an 18-year-old would acquire this book during freshman year in college. I would hope they would read the whole book early in their journey as a student but perhaps hold on to it and reread sections two and three after launching their careers. I hope it will be a book they keep and refer to from time to time—even later in their careers.

The Book's Format

I have, by design, kept the chapters of the book short, typically no more than a dozen pages or less. The entire book is only about 150 pages. This was also intentional. I recognize that students and early-career professionals have extremely busy lives, and their time is precious. I didn't want to write a 300-page volume that the reader might never finish. This approach required me to prioritize the most important topics and endeavor to cover the key points succinctly.

At the beginning of each chapter, I have highlighted the "Key Takeaway" from the chapter. The intent is to let the reader know the most important concept or advice right up front before delving into details. Each chapter also includes an anecdote describing something I experienced during my career that illustrates the guidance in that chapter in a real-world way.

Each chapter also includes "Food for Thought," a quotation that reinforces the advice that precedes it. It was fun selecting these quotations, which come from the worlds of business, sports, politics, and history.

One last observation: Although the book can certainly be read from start to finish, I believe the format also lends itself to being used as a reference tool. For instance, a reader who wants to focus on the importance of relationships can refer to Chapter 14 without having read the preceding 13 chapters. This feature may be particularly helpful to those looking for a refresher on certain topics.

My hope is that this format will add to the readability and usefulness of the book.

Your Feedback Is Welcome

One piece of advice I offer in the pages that follow is "always ask for feedback." So, I would be remiss if I did not follow my own advice. Your comments, suggestions and advice on how to improve the book are welcome. If there is a second edition, I will certainly consider incorporating your input. Comments can be sent to jerrymaginnis@outlook.com.

Jerry Maginnis

May 17, 2021

Navigating Your Route to a Rewarding Accounting Career

CHAPTER ONE

Why Accounting Is a Great Profession

Key Takeaway

Accounting is a terrific profession that can both create an excellent standard of living for you and your family and challenge you to grow, professionally and personally. It can develop and position you for many exciting career opportunities while simultaneously offering a sense of purpose and satisfaction.

Some high school or college students do extensive research before deciding to major in accounting. Others may be steered in that direction by family members or friends in the profession. A few, perhaps, just happen to make a lucky choice. But if you have chosen accounting as your major in college, regardless of how you got to that point, congratulations! You have, in my opinion, made an excellent decision!

There are many reasons accounting is a wonderful profession; here are some of the most compelling:

✓ The work is interesting, challenging and meaningful and provides a platform for you to make an impact.

✓ Launching your career in accounting can position you for a variety of excellent opportunities as your career progresses.

✓ Every organization needs someone with strong accounting skills and experience. The profession offers the potential to advise or be part of a senior leadership team in whatever environment or industry you choose to work.

✓ The financial rewards can be significant.

✓ The profession offers a great deal of flexibility.

✓ The sense of purpose and "psychic" rewards can be powerful as well.

Let's take a closer look at each of these points.

Challenging Work

Accountants are charged with mastering a body of business and professional knowledge that is significant in scope and often complex. The rules are constantly evolving to keep pace with rapidly changing business, technology, and regulatory landscapes. Even after you have a good grasp of the necessary concepts and requirements, professional judgment is required to appropriately apply that guidance to complex business transactions and situations. The accounting profession offers many opportunities for continuous growth, learning and personal development. Because you will be constantly learning new things, you'll find the work interesting and rewarding. These factors will contribute to your value as a professional. Contrary to the perception some people have about accounting being boring or routine, my experience is that professional accountants are constantly challenged to stay current and deal with interesting transactions and events that keep them on the leading edge of a fast-moving business environment.

A Pathway to Other Opportunities

A background in accounting is a valuable asset for any corporate leader, especially one charged with managing a business. A good friend of mine joined a major accounting firm upon graduating from college. He worked with the firm about four years on the audit staff, passed the Certified Public Accountant (CPA) exam, and then joined an insurance firm in an accounting role. That company wound up being part of CIGNA Corporation, a Fortune 100 Company,[1] and my friend, Ed Hanway, eventually became the chief executive officer (CEO) of CIGNA. I'm confident Ed's background and experience as an accountant and CPA were extremely valuable to him when he took on that significant leadership role. I have seen quite a few other examples of individuals who started in accounting

---

[1] CIGNA was ranked number 13 by total revenue on the 2021 Fortune 500 list of the largest U.S. corporations. *Fortune* (2 June) https://fortune.com/company/cigna/fortune500/

and became members of senior management teams or board members of public and private companies. The bottom line: You can have many different "careers" within your accounting career.

Because companies and organizations of all sizes, in all industries, regardless of where they are located geographically, require the skills and experiences of accountants to be successful, the potential opportunities for individuals in this field are wide ranging and diverse. Your accounting degree and skills can take you just about anywhere you choose to go!

Seat at the Table

Every organization, from a Fortune 500 company with global operations to a small nonprofit, needs to understand its financial position and results of operations. Organizations need to budget and manage cash flows, raise funds to enable growth, and allocate capital effectively and efficiently to achieve their objectives. They need the help and active involvement of accountants to be successful. So, accountants are typically "in the room" when important business decisions are considered, and many times are the ones recommending a given course of action or serving as a key advisor to a senior leadership team. Examples include making major investments such as launching a new product line or building a plant, or perhaps advising senior management on how to raise debt or equity capital needed for a company to achieve its objectives. Good CEOs and business leaders understand the importance of the numbers and typically do not make major decisions without soliciting the advice and input of their accounting team. As famed investor Warren Buffett has said: "Accounting is the language of business."[2]

Financial Rewards

Salaries and benefits associated with entry-level positions, particularly at the largest accounting firms, are extremely competitive compared to those of college graduates in other disciplines. The potential for increased compensation as your career progresses is also outstanding when compared to other professions. Over my career, I was actively involved in setting compensation levels for professionals at my firm. While there were some

---

[2] CNBC interview with Buffett, July 31, 2014.

ebbs and flows, often related to the state of the economy, top performers were routinely rewarded with double-digit raises and bonuses. The opportunities were even better for those who became CPAs. When people left positions in public accounting, it was often for significant increases in compensation. Chief financial officers (CFOs) of publicly traded companies are typically among the highest paid executives at their companies. In summary, accounting is one of the better-compensated professions.

I haven't included salary information here because it would quickly become out of date. A quick internet search is an effective way to understand compensation potential, since certain organizations publish annual salary guides with up-to-date market information.

Flexibility

Most jobs in accounting certainly have "busy seasons" associated with deadlines for tax returns or financial reporting requirements. But firms typically try to strike a balance with their overall time-off policies. Potential employers often offer five to six weeks of paid time off (a combination of vacation, sick leave, personal days, etc.) to new hires. These same employers offer six to eight paid holidays annually and often shut down for a week or so around the holidays (with pay). Extended time off for new parents is an increasingly common benefit. As your career progresses, you tend to have more control over your own schedule. Also, as the profession embraces technology, more people are working remotely, including from their homes when circumstances permit. This trend has accelerated because of the COVID-19 pandemic. Many accountants choose to start their own firms, giving them total control over their schedules. In short, accounting is a career that can offer a great degree of flexibility!

Purpose-driven Rewards

Most young people today are looking for more than a financially rewarding job. They also want a role that provides a sense of purpose and offers psychological rewards; a sense of personal satisfaction that what they are doing every day is important work that contributes to society. The accounting profession offers this sense of purpose in a meaningful way. Accountants play a particularly important role in the efficient functioning of the capital markets by ensuring investors and creditors have timely and accurate financial information to make important decisions. This contributes to the efficient allocation of capital, which directly affects the health and vitality of our economy and the well-being of every U.S. citizen. It is also an important responsibility. When Enron (if you are not familiar with it, you will be learning in one of your early accounting classes about how its inaccurate financial reporting misled investors) and other major U.S. companies failed in the early 2000s after a series of accounting scandals, the stock market dropped precipitously and the overall economy was damaged, hurting many people and their families.[3]

But What's the Bottom Line?

All the above potential opportunities may sound attractive, but it is most important that you ENJOY what you do. Work and career are for a long time, in some cases 40 years or longer. No one wants to do something every day they don't enjoy, and, arguably, no one should have to work at a job that they are merely tolerating, even if the pay is good. Rather, they should strive to find a role they can be passionate about—a job that is interesting, exciting and offers continuous learning opportunities and challenges. Accounting isn't for everybody, but the opportunities are wide open for those who enjoy it and are willing to proactively take advantage of all the potential rewards it offers.

Myth—Accountants Are Introverts

Some people believe accountants tend to be introverted—quiet and shy by nature. Popular culture often depicts them as such. I find this to be a sweeping generalization that is often inaccurate. During my career, I met and interacted with many accounting professionals who I would describe as dynamic, funny, innovative, friendly, outgoing, and charismatic. So, forget those stereotypes!

---

[3] Altraide, D. (2019). "Enron, The Biggest Fraud in History." ColdFusion TV. (YouTube). www.youtube.com/watch?v=e5qC1YGRMKI

The Difference Between Public and Private Accounting

Students often ask me about this topic and the answer is simple. If you are in public accounting, you are performing work for a client and your firm (which could be global, regional or local) is billing that client for your services. If you work in private accounting, you are working directly for your employer, usually within their accounting department. Your employer could be a publicly traded company, a private business or a non-profit organization.

How I Chose Accounting

Why did I choose the accounting profession? I'd like to tell you it was the result of doing careful and thoughtful research about the best career path given my interests and aptitudes. But that would not be true. The honest answer is that my understanding was that accounting was a good field if you wanted to be confident you could find and keep a job after graduating from college.

During my high school years, the U.S. economy was struggling, hampered by high rates of inflation and high unemployment. So, finding and keeping a job was especially important to me. This was the primary driver in my decision to give accounting a try. While my basic premise proved to be accurate, I was fortunate because it turned out I found the work interesting and challenging. I wound up being actively engaged in the profession for my entire career. Based on my experience, and for all the good reasons detailed above, I feel confident in encouraging young people to pursue careers in accounting.

Food for Thought

Your work is going to fill a large part of your life, and the only way to be truly satisfied is to do what you believe is great work. And the only way to do great work is to love what you do.

—Steve Jobs, founder of Apple

CHAPTER TWO

Is Becoming a CPA the Right Path for You?

 ### Key Takeaway

Investing the time and effort to become a CPA, preferably immediately after earning your accounting degree, will significantly improve your career prospects and earnings potential. There are other valuable credentials available to accountants that can supplement or be an alternative to a CPA designation. If you decide not to pursue a CPA path, consider obtaining an advanced degree and one of these other credentials.

Many accountants have achieved significant career success without becoming a certified public accountant. You can do well financially and obtain high-level, rewarding positions of responsibility in major corporations without becoming a CPA. That said, I believe that you considerably increase your probability of a successful career in accounting if you do become a CPA. In many cases, CPAs will earn more over their careers than accountants who don't possess the credential. Some estimate that the designation will help you earn an extra $1 million over the course of your career. CPAs as a group also tend to be offered more and better job opportunities than non-CPAs. If that's true, why wouldn't everyone strive to become a CPA? The answer is that it requires a significant investment of time, effort, and resources over and above what is required to simply earn an accounting degree.

What Is the Difference Between a Regular Accountant and a CPA?

A typical college accounting degree requires 120 credit hours, the equivalent of four years of study. Becoming a CPA requires 150 credit hours of postsecondary education, the equivalent of an extra year of study, plus passing a rigorous four-part examination and meeting minimum experience requirements. CPA licenses are granted by individual state boards of accountancy. Although the CPA examination is standard across all states, other requirements, particularly related to experience, can vary from state to state. Once an accountant has earned the certification, most jurisdictions require a minimum number of continuing education hours on a periodic basis to maintain the license.[4]

Beyond the additional time and cost of the extra 30 credit hours, there are costs associated with studying for and passing the CPA exam. There is a fee to take the exam itself, but the biggest cost is for a CPA exam preparation course. Although it is possible to pass the exam without taking such a course, it makes the task much harder. I recommend that CPA exam aspirants invest in a prep class. Costs of prep courses vary, as do their quality, but can exceed $3,000. Finally, the incremental study time required to prepare for and pass the exam can be substantial. Again, the time required will vary from one person to the next, but 350 to 450 hours would not be unusual.

While all this may sound a little daunting, keep in mind that your CPA is the entrance ticket to a highly respected profession and will open the door to many opportunities for the rest of your career. Also, many firms and companies offer reimbursement for some or all the costs associated with passing the CPA exam.

Although there are a variety of professional designations available for accountants (more on this below), my opinion is that the CPA is the best known and most well-respected credential. It has evolved into a brand of its own and conveys trust, independence, and credibility. Many business-people as well as the "man or woman on the street" think of a CPA as a professional with special skills and expertise, and the public perception of the designation is extremely positive. I would wager a lot of money that

---

[4] AICPA (see www.thiswaytocpa.com)

it is better-known than any of the accounting credentials discussed below, perhaps because it has also been around longer than just about all of them (about 125 years at this point). Ironically, many people associate the CPA with tax-preparation services even though it is more important for auditors than tax accountants to have a CPA certificate.

The CPA designation can be useful and helpful in a variety of potential career paths, but it is absolutely essential if you intend to pursue an auditing career in public accounting because virtually all jurisdictions mandate that only a licensed CPA can sign an audit report. The designation also enables you to represent clients with the Internal Revenue Service, which is helpful for certain tax professionals.

If you desire to pursue the CPA, it's important to understand the 150-hour requirement very early in your college years and to develop a game plan on how you'll achieve the extra 30 credit hours (see Chapter 3 for more on this point). In making this decision, keep in mind that many high schools' Advanced Placement (AP) classes qualify for college credit, giving you a head start on the extra credit hours. Also, you can take classes at a community college as a cost-effective way to earn the extra credits.

How Do I Decide Whether to Pursue 150 Credit Hours?

The 150 credit hours required for a CPA may not be for everyone. Let's look at the pros and cons of pursuing it.

Pros:
- ✓ Additional education is valuable, particularly if it is in courses relevant to your field.
- ✓ Achieving 150 credit hours will qualify you to become a CPA.
- ✓ Becoming a CPA could result in increased earnings potential and better job opportunities.

Cons:
- ✓ The extra 30 credits have a cost, both in terms of time and money.
- ✓ Part of the "time" cost is that you may be delayed from taking a full-time job, resulting in lost earnings potential (an "opportunity cost").
- ✓ The additional tuition for the extra 30 credits could increase your student loan debt burden.

Other important considerations to think about in making the decision:

✓ Do I intend to pursue a career in the audit profession? If so, you will need to ultimately be licensed to perform attest services and the CPA will be necessary for career success.

✓ While the CPA is "nice to have," it is not required to provide tax or advisory services.

✓ Similarly, a CPA is not required for the certain jobs available outside the public accounting arena, including many positions in the corporate, government or nonprofit sectors.

Timing

Some accountants have obtained their extra 30 credits and passed the CPA exam many years after graduating from college, so it is possible to do it a bit later in life. Nonetheless, my advice, if you aspire to become a CPA, is to pursue the extra credits and pass the exam sooner rather than later. Taking the exam shortly after graduating from college is optimum. This is because, as a practical matter, it can become more challenging to find the time to study and pass the exam as the years go by and you take on more professional and personal responsibilities. Also, having just completed college, you're accustomed to preparing for and passing exams. Why not take advantage of those skills before they get rusty?

Myth—The CPA Exam Is Too Hard and Not Worth the Effort

I often hear students complain that the CPA exam requires too much time, effort and cost and therefore, they don't intend to pursue a CPA path. But the fact that there are more than a half-million CPAs in America today is proof that the exam is not "too hard." If that many people passed it, you can too! Yes, the exam does require a fair amount of study time. But you'll realize the benefits of your investment of that time for the rest of your working career. In terms of the CPA being "worth it," you will increase your earnings potential and job opportunities for decades to come with those letters behind your name! Becoming a CPA is a high return on investment (ROI) proposition.

The CPA Evolution Project

As I write these words in Spring 2021, the American Institute of Certified Public Accountants (AICPA) and the National Association of State Boards of Accountancy (NASBA) are working on a joint initiative to transform the CPA licensure model to recognize the rapidly changing skills and competencies accountancy requires today and will require in the future. They have proposed moving to a "core + discipline" CPA licensure model. Under this scenario, CPA candidates would be required to complete the same robust core education and examination in accounting, auditing, tax and technology plus choose a discipline in which to demonstrate deeper knowledge. The three potential disciplines being considered reflect three pillars of the profession:

✓ Business reporting and analysis

✓ Information systems and controls

✓ Tax compliance and planning

Final recommendations for the Evolution project are expected in mid- to late 2021, followed by a multiyear implementation plan. Aspiring CPAs will want to monitor developments related to the Evolution project.

Other Credentials

There are numerous professional certifications and credentials that you can pursue after earning your accounting degree, but it can get a bit confusing to distinguish one from another and evaluate their value in the marketplace. Let's take a look at some credentialing opportunities beyond the CPA designation, understand what is involved in achieving them and assess how they might benefit you.

✓ **Certified Management Accountant (CMA)**—To earn the CMA, you must meet the following requirements: 1) hold an active IMA (Institute of Management Accountants) membership; 2) complete and pass parts 1 and 2 of the CMA exam; 3) hold a bachelor's degree from an accredited college or university or a related professional certification; 4) abide by IMA's Statement of Ethical Professional Practice, and 5) have two continuous years of professional experience in management accounting or financial management.[5] A CMA designation would be most valuable to someone planning a career in management accounting.

✓ **Chartered Global Management Accountant (CGMA)**—To achieve a CGMA designation, you need to complete the CGMA Finance Leadership program and pass an exam. You must also be a member of the AICPA in good standing and have a minimum of three years of relevant, work-based, practical management accounting experience.[6] Like the CMA, the CGMA would be most relevant and useful to individuals pursuing careers in management accounting.

✓ **Certified Fraud Examiner (CFE)**—Before applying to become a CFE, you must meet the following criteria: 1) be a member in good standing of the Association of Certified Fraud Examiners (ACFE); 2) meet minimum academic and professional requirements; 3) be of high moral character, and 4) agree to abide by the Bylaws and Code of Professional Ethics of the ACFE. CFE aspirants must also pass an exam that tests knowledge and expertise in the four primary areas of fraud examination: 1) Financial transactions and fraud schemes; 2) Law; 3) Investigation, and 4) Fraud prevention and deterrence.[7] A CFE may be useful if you are considering a career as a forensic accountant. Potential employers might include accounting firms with a forensic practice, a company with a sizable internal audit department or a government agency such as the Federal Bureau of Investigation.

✓ **Certified Internal Auditor (CIA)**—The Institute of Internal Auditors (IIA) requires a bachelor's degree and 24 months of internal audit work experience (or a master's degree and 12 months of internal audit experience). Aspirants must also exhibit high moral and professional character, pass an examination, and agree to abide by the IIA's Code of Ethics.[8] A CIA would be most relevant and helpful for those pursuing careers as internal audit professionals.

---

[5] IMA(see www.imanet.org)

[6] AICPA (on AICPA.org, search CGMA Designation)

[7] Association of Certified Fraud Examiners, Inc. (acfe.com/cfe-qualifications.aspx)

[8] The Institute of Internal Auditors (theiia.org)

✓ **Certified Information Systems Auditor (CISA)**—The CISA designation is for those interested in information systems auditing, control and security. To earn it, you must meet the following requirements: 1) successful completion of the CISA examination; 2) submit an application for CISA certification; 3) adhere to the Code of Professional Ethics; 4) adhere to the continuing professional education requirements, and 5) comply with the Information Systems Auditing Standards.[9] The CISA designation is appropriate for an audit professional focused on IT controls and cybersecurity risk.

✓ **Certified Bank Auditor (CBA)**—To become a CBA, you must possess a bachelor's degree in accounting, complete a four-part multiple-choice exam in less than three years and have at least two years of professional bank auditing experience.[10] This credential may be of interest to those contemplating a career in the financial services industry.

✓ **Enrolled Agent (EA)**—Enrolled agents have earned the privilege of representing taxpayers before the Internal Revenue Service by either passing a three-part comprehensive IRS test covering individual and business tax returns, or through experience as a former IRS employee. Enrolled agent status is the highest credential the IRS awards. Individuals who obtain this status must adhere to ethical standards and complete 72 hours of continuing education courses every three years.[11] As implied by the requirements, an EA designation would be most helpful and relevant for professionals who want to represent clients before the IRS, usually in matters involving tax disputes.

✓ **Certified Government Financial Manager (CGFM)**—The CGFM certification is awarded by the Association of Government Accountants (AGA) for demonstrating competency in governmental accounting, auditing, financial reporting, internal controls, and budgeting at the federal, state and local levels. To earn the CGFM, you must complete an online application and read and agree to abide

---

[9] ISACA (www.isaca.org/Certification/CISA-Certified-Information-Systems-Auditor/How-to-become-certified/Pages/default.aspx)

[10] Investopedia.com (www.investopedia.com/terms/c/cba.asp)

[11] Internal Revenue Service (www.irs.gov/tax-professionals/enrolled-agents/enrolled-agent-information)

by the AGA's Code of Ethics. You must also have a bachelor's degree in any subject area from an accredited U.S. college or university, pass three comprehensive CFGM examinations and have at least two years of professional-level experience in government financial management.[12]

Is That It?

Nope. The credentials covered above aren't all of those available. But they represent a sampling of what's out there. My intent is to illustrate that there are many options, and you'll want to thoughtfully consider what is best for you. The AICPA alone offers the following credentials in addition to the CPA and CGMA noted above: 1) Personal Financial Specialist (PFS); 2) Certified in Financial Forensics (CFF); 3) Accredited in Business Valuation (ABV); 4) Certified Information Technology Professional (CITP), and 5) Certified in Entity and Intangible Valuations (CEIV). By the way, each of these credentials, with the exception of the CEIV, requires that you be a CPA to earn the designation. So, your CPA certificate can provide the opportunity to further specialize in the future. Several of the other organizations mentioned above also offer credentials beyond the primary ones I've described.

The credentials can be confusing, so do your homework before choosing a path to follow.

What About Advanced Degrees?

Education is extremely important to success in any field today, but this is particularly true of the accounting profession. Depending on your career path, a master's in business administration, master's in tax or accounting, or other advanced degree can be helpful to your success. This is just my opinion, but I think a college degree today is the equivalent of a high school diploma 30 or 40 years ago. It's nice to have but won't necessarily set you apart. Whether you pursue one or more credentials or advanced degrees, recognize that continuous learning and growth are essential to success in the accounting profession.

---

[12] The Association of Government Accountants (www.aga.cgfm.org)

Return on Investment (ROI)

All credentials have a cost. There are fees to take the qualifying exam and, quite likely, a review course. There may be ongoing costs to maintain the credential after you've earned it, such as fees for continuing education classes or license renewals. But the biggest cost is usually the time (typically hundreds of hours) you'll invest to pass the exam required for the credential. Of course, you should expect a return on the investment you are making in yourself. While the cost to obtain a credential may seem significant when you are just starting out, it will likely ultimately prove to be very small when you consider that you'll enjoy the benefits of the credential for decades to come. In my own case, I feel strongly that deciding to become a CPA was one of the best decisions I ever made, and the cost was nominal compared to the significant benefits I have derived from becoming a CPA.

Give some serious and thoughtful consideration to this ROI analysis as you evaluate the credentialing options and career path you plan to take.

So, What's My Advice?

I confess that my opinion is influenced by my own experience, but I strongly recommend that every accountant seriously consider becoming a CPA. Depending on the ultimate career path you pursue, it may be a good idea to supplement your CPA with one of the other credentials mentioned above.

My Experience Pursuing the CPA

I passed the CPA exam early in my career. I didn't keep precise records of the time I invested attending preparation classes and studying but I would estimate it at 400 hours. It was a challenging year. I didn't see as much of my friends or my girlfriend, Lee Ann (who later became my wife), as I would have liked. As I reflect on that year now, however, I realize it was the best investment I ever made in my own development. When I evaluate the financial and other benefits that I've derived from being a CPA over my career, it's clear that the payback received on my investment of money and study time has been substantial. The sacrifices I made that year were well worth the long-term benefits!

Food for Thought

A career is something that you train for and prepare for and plan on doing for a long time.

—Sonia Sotomayor, Associate Justice,
    U.S. Supreme Court

CHAPTER THREE

How Accounting Majors Can Optimize Their College Experience

Key Takeaway

If you've decided to major in accounting, there are some specific, practical things you can do, starting at the outset of your freshman year, that will help you make the most of your time on campus and position you for excellent career opportunities.

Sadly, I have observed far too many accounting students learn too late in their college experience about resources that could have helped them and opportunities they ideally would have taken advantage of, had they been aware of them. The result, often, is a sense of frustration and regret on the part of those students. I hear them say, "If only I had known, I would have handled things differently." This chapter is intended to acquaint accounting majors with the things they should know about early in their university experience—ideally in the beginning of freshman year.

Before we dive into my "Top 10" list, it's worth mentioning—and emphasizing—the importance of achieving your academic potential. You are at your college or university to learn, so make it a point to pursue academic excellence! While your grades are not necessarily a predictor of your future success, they are incredibly important in positioning you for the best opportunities. I tell students all the time that someone with a grade point average (GPA) of 3.5 or higher is probably going to be more sought after than a student with a 2.5 GPA. You might feel that it's "not fair," but it is how the world works. The good news is that you can control your own destiny by being organized and studying hard!

The 10 tips that follow are very much interrelated. For example, the resources in the Career Center can be helpful in preparing your resume.

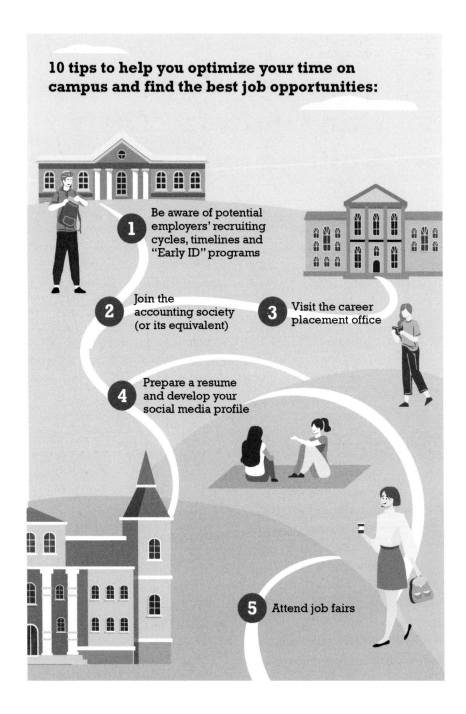

10 tips to help you optimize your time on campus and find the best job opportunities:

1. Be aware of potential employers' recruiting cycles, timelines and "Early ID" programs

2. Join the accounting society (or its equivalent)

3. Visit the career placement office

4. Prepare a resume and develop your social media profile

5. Attend job fairs

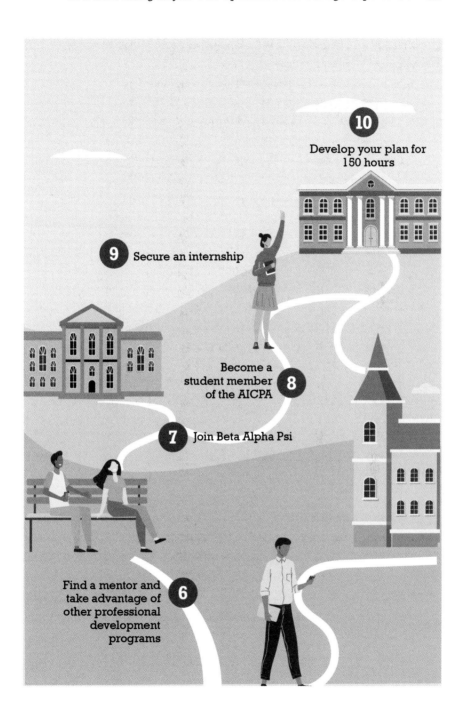

10 Develop your plan for 150 hours

9 Secure an internship

Become a student member of the AICPA 8

7 Join Beta Alpha Psi

Find a mentor and take advantage of other professional development programs 6

Understanding recruiting cycles can be key to landing an internship. Consequently, the list should not be viewed as being in chronological or priority order. As a general observation, many of them should be addressed during your freshman year or early in your sophomore year. The key is being aware of and tapping into the resources available to you. In this regard, another good step for a new student is to talk with some juniors and seniors. Most will be happy to assist if you ask for their advice, and you'll get the benefit of their experience when they share what they've learned.

Here are the 10 tips to help you optimize your time on campus and find the best job opportunities:

1—Be aware of potential employers' recruiting cycles, timelines and "Early ID" programs

Some students naively think they don't need to focus on getting a job until senior year. The reality is that competition for the top positions is intense and begins the day you set foot on campus. The largest accounting firms and many other high-caliber companies focus on identifying talent early in a student's academic journey. They want to meet you as a freshman, potentially invite you to get to know their firm and people as a sophomore through "externship" and "inside look" programs and then offer you an internship during your junior year. If that goes well, they will seek to lock you up with a full-time job offer before you even start your senior year (even though your start date might be 15 months away). This is an incredibly accelerated recruiting cycle and, if you're not aware of it, you can miss out on some great opportunities.

2—Join the accounting society (or its equivalent)

Most colleges and universities have a "club" for accounting majors. Called the accounting society or something similar, these organizations are student-led and typically meet six to eight times over the course of a semester. They have guest speakers from firms or companies that are potential employers and are active in recruiting at the school. The presentations deal with important subjects such as career paths in public and private accounting, how to prepare a resume, how to get ready for a job interview, etc. These are topics students need to become familiar with early in their time on campus, so these talks offer terrific learning opportunities. They also provide a chance to get to know and build relationships with potential employers that may want to hire you. In my experience, the most highly motivated and engaged students tend to seek out leadership roles in these student clubs. The clubs typically have five or six elected officers, positions that can further enhance the student experience and the opportunity to build relationships.

3—Visit the career placement office

Universities generally have some type of career placement office, and they may have one specifically associated with and focused on students in their business schools. This is a great place to learn about resources and opportunities. Placement offices often also offer programming (workshops, seminars, etc.) to familiarize students with the basics of finding internships and after-graduation jobs: researching employers, dressing appropriately for an interview, communicating with prospective employers, and so on.

4—Prepare a resume and develop your social media profile

Many students don't have a resume when they start their college experience. You should prepare one early in your academic journey and update it regularly. Your placement office often is willing to help with this process. The mere act of preparing a resume can prompt you to consider how you "look on paper" and steps you can take to round out your profile (activities, student leadership roles, etc.).

It's also important for college students to have a business-oriented social media presence. I recommend developing your LinkedIn profile and becoming familiar with this tool early in your time on campus. Use it proactively to connect with recruiters and prospective employers. Make sure you obtain a professional headshot photo and keep your profile up to date as you complete additional courses and become involved in campus activities. And be aware that your social media posts—not just on LinkedIn, but on any site—can have a long life and reflect either poorly or well on how others view you.

5—Attend job fairs

Students often assume that job fairs are for seniors who will be graduating within a year and therefore don't take the time to attend them during their first two or three years on campus. This is a mistake. Accounting firms and companies that recruit at these events offer internships that are available junior year or sooner. I advise students to start attending these events during their second year at school. Even though you may not yet be "in the job market," attending will give you a feel for what takes place and enable you to start building relationships with prospective employers that may pay off in the future. These events also give you an opportunity to develop a relationship with individual recruiters who sometimes are willing to offer advice on steps you can take to become a more competitive candidate.

6—Find a mentor and take advantage of other professional development programs

Whether within the accounting program itself or through the business school's career placement office, universities usually offer programs that help prepare students to transition into the workforce.

Mentoring programs are particularly valuable in that they pair students with alumni or other professionals connected with the university who are willing to coach and help develop students. These interactions are also a form of networking that can result in job leads or other opportunities. In addition, a good mentor can provide valuable advice and coaching that will help you make the transition from being a student to entering the workforce.

Mock interviews and similar programs will sharpen your interview skills by letting you practice in a friendly environment that offers you feedback and tips on how to improve, setting you up for success in "real" interviews.

7—Join Beta Alpha Psi

Beta Alpha Psi (BAP)[13] is the premier organization for students majoring in accounting and seeking to enter the profession in the near term. It is an honors organization and requires a minimum grade point average. You also need to have completed your Intermediate Accounting class and are expected to attend a minimum number of meetings each semester and participate in service activities. Taking part will yield many benefits, including exposure to a variety of professionals and firms. Presentations at BAP chapters typically focus on topics that will enhance your technical knowledge and prepare you to be a professional. The organization also hosts regional and annual meetings that provide opportunities to expand your network and hear from high-profile speakers and leaders in the accounting profession.

8—Become a student member of the AICPA

The AICPA is a professional membership organization for CPAs and management accountants. Joining is easy to do at no cost to you. The Institute gives you access to what is going on in the profession and to a variety of resources and thought leadership pieces.[14] You may also want to consider joining your state CPA Society. Most of these have some form of student membership available at no cost.

9—Secure an internship

Nothing beats getting some practical work experience in your field. Importantly, it can help you to validate the career path you've chosen. Many students are doing internships after their second year of college. Do some research to learn what internships are available and make sure you understand which courses you need to have completed to qualify for the opportunity. Also, be aware that internships often lead to offers of full-time employment. This is certainly the recruiting model followed by many accounting firms and certain corporate employers. Even if an internship doesn't result in a full-time job opportunity after graduation

---

[13] Beta Alpha Psi (www.bap.org)

[14] AICPA (www.thiswaytocpa.com/join-aicpa/)

with the same employer, it will look good on your resume and position you for other attractive job opportunities by helping develop your skills. Plus, there are financial benefits from internships as the compensation can be better than certain other part-time jobs students typically take while attending school. Finally, understand that students who graduate with no prior accounting-oriented work experience can sometimes be at a disadvantage in finding their first position after graduation.

10—Develop your plan for 150 hours

As discussed in Chapter Two, to become licensed as a CPA you must have 150 credit hours. The typical undergraduate program offers 15 credit hours (five three-credit courses) per semester or 30 per year, so many students graduate with 120 credit hours, satisfying the school's minimum requirements for a B.S. degree in accounting. Most of the larger accounting firms have a strong preference to hire students who are aware of these circumstances and have planned accordingly, positioning themselves to graduate with 150 credit hours before starting full-time employment, whether that be in four years or five years.

Requirements regarding the subject matter the extra 30 credit hours must cover vary from State to State but students will generally benefit from taking the extra credits in classes that cover accounting, auditing or tax topics. Careful consideration should be given to which classes to take. Maybe you want to select certain electives that will help you get an overall well-rounded education. To better prepare for your career some good options would include classes dealing with Data Analytics, Predictive Analytics, Systems and Organization Controls, Digital Acumen, Cybersecurity, IT Audit, IT Governance and IT Risks and Controls, based on a report released by the AICPA and the National Association of State Boards of Accountancy in Spring 2021.[15]

---

[15] See Accounting Program Curriculum Gap Analysis available at www.aicpa.org

There are many strategies for achieving the extra 30 credit hours. Here are a few to consider:

✓ Take one extra class per semester (over 8 semesters, this will earn you 24 "extra" credits). Add in a couple of classes in the summer months or "winter" semesters (between fall and spring) that some schools offer, and you could graduate with 150 hours in four years. This approach creates a consistently heavy workload, which may not be feasible for students involved in sports or other extracurricular activities or holding down part-time jobs. But it's a strategy that can work well for others who are able to focus primarily on academics. A potential additional attraction of this approach is that some institutions permit students to take extra credits in a semester for the same tuition cost as 15 credits.

✓ Take online classes over the summers or on winter breaks (often offered on a condensed schedule basis).

✓ Take extra classes at a local community college (again, a potentially cost-effective approach).

✓ Consider obtaining the extra credits via a dual major or a minor in another discipline (Accounting and Finance is one combination that has been popular traditionally; Accounting and Management Information Systems (MIS) may be a better choice prospectively).

✓ Consider a five-year program that enables you to leave school with a B.S. in accounting, a Master of Business Administration (MBA) degree and the 150 credits you need to be CPA-eligible.

✓ Similarly, consider a Master in Accountancy program (MAC), offered at many institutions, which typically requires a fifth year in school. Some MAC programs have a focus on preparing students to take and pass the CPA exam shortly after graduation.

✓ In recent years, certain universities have begun to offer a Master in Data Analytics program; this is another option that is particularly attractive in the current environment.

My Teacher and Mentor

I attended Saint Joseph's University in Philadelphia. There was an accounting professor there named Ed Sutula. Professor Sutula taught Principles of Accounting in the fall of my freshman year and I liked him a lot. He was a practicing CPA (he taught in the mornings and ran his CPA practice in the afternoon) and so had the ability to explain the material in a way that helped me understand its real-world application. He also had a great sense of humor. I'm not sure whether it was coincidental or if I again got lucky, but it turned out that Professor Sutula happened to be teaching whatever accounting course I needed to take each semester for most of my college years. Because I liked him so much, I kept enrolling in his classes, including Intermediate Accounting, Tax, and Cost Accounting. In total, I think he taught seven of my eight required accounting classes during my time at Saint Joe's. He had a powerful and very favorable impact on me. He was both a fine teacher and a great role model. Make it a point to get to know your professors and maybe you'll find your own Ed Sutula!

Lesson Learned: Mentors are important to your career success. Make it a priority to find them!

Food for Thought

I will prepare and someday, my chance will come.

—Abraham Lincoln

CHAPTER FOUR

Career Paths

Key Takeaway

There are many desirable career paths available for individuals possessing an accounting degree. Make the time to understand your options and think about your preferences.

The really great thing about accounting is that virtually every organization needs the skills, capabilities, and services of accounting professionals. Every business, large or small, needs, at a minimum, to file a tax return, requiring it to maintain a set of accounting records. Many also need to prepare financial statements subject to external audit to be provided to investors, creditors, or regulatory agencies. Perhaps most important, business owners need to understand how their businesses are performing and a good accountant can facilitate financial analysis and assist with necessary operational corrections. These circumstances apply to global, sophisticated Fortune 500 companies as well as small businesses like your neighborhood dry cleaners or pizza shop. Nonprofit and government organizations are also required to maintain accounting records and, ideally, use them to guide strategic decisions.

All these organizations either need to employ accountants directly or to engage an accounting firm or other consultants to assist them in meeting their responsibilities. As a result, accountants work in every industry you can think of, from internet and software companies to the worlds of sports and entertainment, fashion, retail, manufacturing, construction, financial services, energy, pharmaceuticals, etc. I could go on, but you get the idea. I stress the breadth of industries because it is important to recognize you may want to focus on a specific industry that you enjoy and where your accounting skills are needed. A good friend of mine, John Nickolas, enjoys sports in general and baseball in particular. John wound up combining that passion and his accounting skills and experience to become the chief financial officer of the Philadelphia Phillies, a job he loves!

Accountants also have significant upward mobility and a variety of career tracks that can be pursued based on their training and experience. Many people will have multiple experiences and roles within their overall career in the accounting profession. Let's review, at a macro level, some of the options available to accountants, starting with types of employers, keeping in mind that you may have the chance to experience several of these positions during your career.

Public Accounting Firms—These firms come in all shapes and sizes, ranging from the Big Four (Deloitte, EY, KPMG, and PwC, the four largest firms in the world) to national, regional, local and sole-proprietor firms. Each type of firm offers advantages and, perhaps, some disadvantages. In general, the larger the firms, the larger the clients. The Big Four firms tend to serve Fortune 1000 companies and global organizations. They have offices and capabilities in many countries because that is necessary to serve such clients. While their clientele also includes larger private and family-owned businesses, most of their revenues are derived from serving publicly owned companies. The Big Four's audit practices are subject to oversight and regulation by the Securities and Exchange Commission (SEC) and Public Company Accounting Oversight Board (PCAOB) in the United States as well as similar regulatory bodies in other countries. *Fortune* magazine has consistently placed all four of the firms on its annual list of "Best Places to Work," citing their excellent formal training programs and very competitive salary and benefits packages, particularly for entry-level hires off college campuses. I may be a bit biased, given my background, but I believe any of the Big Four firms would be a great place to begin a career. The learning and growth opportunities available in these environments are truly world class.

Myth—If I Don't Start with a Big Four Firm Coming Out of School, It Will Hurt My Career

While joining a Big Four firm right out of college is a great way to launch your career, starting elsewhere doesn't mean that your future will be negatively affected. I have known many people who did not start with a large firm and still enjoyed remarkably successful careers. Some of them never worked in public accounting at all. Many had terrific careers in government or the nonprofit sector. Some of them started with smaller firms or in industry and later became partners at one of the Big Four firms.

Although the Big Four have much to offer, other public accounting firms also provide great opportunities. Some, like Grant Thornton, BDO, and RSM (sometimes referred to as "the next tier"), also operate globally, serve an important segment of the market and recruit at many colleges and universities.

Certain firms provide a culture and work environment that some professionals may prefer over that of a Big Four firm. The nature of other firms' practices can vary widely, but many serve challenging and interesting clients. National and regional firms serve both publicly and privately owned companies, although they tend to be smaller than those served by the Big Four. Many of the clients of firms outside the Big Four operate in what is referred to as the "middle market." Local firms and sole proprietors tend to serve smaller, family-owned businesses and individuals and may derive a meaningful portion of their revenues from tax and accounting services.

Within public accounting firms of all sizes, there are three primary businesses: audit, tax and consulting (sometimes referred to as advisory services). Let's take a closer look at each of these practice areas.

Audit involves providing third-party assurance that a client's financial statements are fairly stated in all material respects. Publicly traded companies are required to obtain an audit and submit their audited financial statements annually to the SEC as part of their form 10-K filing. Companies in many other regulated industries (e.g., banking, insurance, etc.) must file audited financial statements with regulators. Private investors and creditors often also require audited financial statements under the terms of their investment or credit agreements. A lesser form of assurance known as a "review" can also be provided, typically by regional or local accounting firms. Some smaller firms will also perform "compilation" services (i.e., assisting their clients in preparing periodic financial statements). To provide audit or assurance services in the United States, firms and individuals must be licensed, typically by their state's board of accountancy. Thus, if you aspire to a career as an auditor, you'll need to obtain your license as a CPA. While it may be helpful to professionals working in tax or advisory practices to also become CPAs, it is a must in the audit business to sign opinions.

While audit is a mature business, it is also a sizable one. The Big Four audit practices generate billions of dollars in fees each year and employ tens of thousands of people. The audit fee for a large global Fortune 100 company can exceed $25 million a year. Many regional and local firms also have well established and profitable audit practices. From a business-model standpoint, one of the positive features of performing audits is that it is an annual recurring service, unless a client company gets acquired or goes out of business. This creates an annuity-like revenue stream for the accounting firm. Many firms have audit clients they have been serving for decades and, in some cases, for over 100 years.

It is particularly important to note that third-party investors and creditors are relying on the work of the independent auditor. As a result, the firms, as well as their partners and employees, must be committed to independence and objectivity in carrying out their work. There is an important reason the "P" in CPA stands for public! Auditors need to understand that third parties are relying on their work and there will be times they need to challenge their client or possibly even resign from an engagement, if warranted by the circumstances. Auditors' impartiality and professional skepticism are critical to their success.

Public accounting firms also provide a variety of tax services that fall into two major categories: compliance, generally involving the preparation or review of tax returns; and consulting, involving tax planning and advice. As with an audit, tax-preparation or compliance services generate a recurring revenue stream since tax returns need to be filed each year. While larger firms perform plenty of tax-compliance services, as a rule, the larger the firm, the more tax planning versus compliance services being provided. As with audits, the larger firms tend to serve the largest, most complex global companies, whereas small firms and sole practitioners usually focus on tax work for individuals or small businesses.

There are myriad types of tax services, including advising on all sorts of tax situations and preparing federal, state and local returns as well as those for foreign countries. Taxes can be extremely complicated and lend themselves to specialization. The largest firms have partners and professionals who specialize in areas such as mergers and acquisitions, partnerships, and transfer pricing, to name just a few. The federal Tax Cuts and Jobs Act of 2017 resulted in a significant amount of incremental business for public accounting firms as their clients scrambled to understand the impact of the new law on their businesses. Congress often enacts new tax legislation—creating an environment in which accountants always have new things to learn and new work to execute.

While audit and tax are "core" services that many firms have been providing for decades, most firms also now offer advisory or consulting services. In fact, advisory has been the fastest-growing business segment for firms of all sizes in the last decade. The consulting practices of several Big Four firms now generate more revenue than their audit practices, even though their audit practices have been around for over 100 years while the consulting businesses, in their current form, started less than 20 years ago.

Accounting firms offer a plethora of consulting or advisory services. Many relate to process and controls or information technology services. Forensic accounting, including fraud investigations, is a growing area, as are business-valuation services. Larger firms employ non-CPA specialists with expertise in other disciplines, such as actuarial science or information technology. From a business-model standpoint, most consulting revenues are engagement-specific or non-recurring, although accounting firms are often successful in developing follow-on work or different types of consulting assignments from clients. Advisory practices at most firms are constantly evolving to respond to marketplace demands. For example, many firms have launched cybersecurity practices in recent years as well as services designed to help companies react to and cope with the COVID-19 pandemic.

One valuable benefit offered by certain public accounting firms is their ability to allow their professionals to transfer from one practice area to another. For instance, someone might start in audit and then move to tax or consulting. In this fashion, it is possible to have multiple career paths while staying at the same firm. Such transfers also enable a firm to retain talent by offering its professionals new, different, and challenging types of assignments. The Big Four and certain other firms also have well-developed rotational assignment opportunities that may involve working in their executive (national) office or spending several years on an international assignment.

Roles You'll Find in Accounting Firms

There are a variety of roles in public accounting firms, and we discuss them below:

Partner—A partner is an owner of the business. A partner's compensation is in the form of a share of a firm's profits as opposed to a salary. As a result, partners are considered self-employed and typically fund their own health care, retirement plan contributions, and employment tax (e.g., Social Security and Medicare) costs. They are usually required to have capital invested (and at risk) in the firm. The amount of a partner's investment is usually tied to the size of the individual's ownership stake and tends to increase over time. If a firm fails, as Andersen did in 2002, partially as a result of the Enron crisis, the partners can lose their invested capital, which is often a material portion of their net worth.

Managing Director (MD)—Some firms have created the MD role in recent years. While MDs have similar responsibilities to partners in certain cases, they are not owners of the business. Certain firms use the term "non-equity" partner for this role. If in the audit practice, the MD may be able to sign audit opinions but only for specified types of entities, like privately owned companies or employee benefit plans. In certain environments, the MD role can be a steppingstone to being promoted to partner. In these instances, while the time a person serves as an MD can vary, it is often three to four years. In other cases, the position is a career role for those who won't be asked to join the partnership.

Senior Manager—Professionals at this level usually have a minimum of seven or eight years of public accounting experience upon being promoted and may spend five or more years in the role. They report to partners or MDs and usually have responsibility for supervising all other professionals working for the firm on an engagement. The position requires strong technical, administrative and management skills, as well as the ability to interact effectively with clients' senior management.

Manager—Most firms require a person to have a minimum of four to five years of experience before being promoted to the manager level. Managers oversee senior and staff accountants and, on a large engagement, may report to a senior manager. On a smaller engagement, the manager may report directly to a partner or MD. Managers often oversee two to three engagements simultaneously and may be interacting with several different clients in a typical week (unless they happen to be assigned to a large engagement or project).

Senior—Sometimes referred to as "in-charge accountants" in the audit practice, these individuals have anywhere from two to four years of experience and are responsible for supervising staff members on a day-to-day basis. They tend to work on one client engagement at a time.

Staff Accountant—The entry-level role at most firms. Most audit professionals and many tax personnel will join a firm upon graduation from university, often after having completed an internship during their time as a student. In recent years, some firms have been hiring fewer entry-level accounting majors because some of their work has been eliminated by new technology, and, in some cases, by the outsourcing or offshoring of tasks historically performed by new hires.

Opportunities in Industry for Accountants

Corporations and Other Businesses—Large companies, such as those in the Fortune 500, can employ hundreds of accountants of their own and offer outstanding career growth opportunities. Most big companies tend to be publicly owned. Accounting positions are also available at mid-size companies, family businesses and start-ups, again and importantly, in virtually every industry. These organizations will hire recent college graduates but also often hire more experienced individuals who have spent time working in public accounting firms. A very typical career path is for someone to start in public accounting out of college and ultimately join a company in industry.

Governments and Nonprofits—Governments also employ tens of thousands of accountants. Positions are available with the federal government as well as state and local government agencies and certain "quasi-government" organizations (like transit agencies and other public authorities). Similarly, the nonprofit sector employs many accountants. As with public accounting firms and industry, the size and sophistication of government and nonprofit organizations vary greatly. Some federal agencies (e.g., Department of Defense) or larger state governments are bigger than a Fortune 500 company in terms of assets and revenues. Similarly, there are large and quite sophisticated healthcare organizations and colleges and universities operating in the nonprofit sector.

There are many job titles and positions available for accountants working in private industry. The following list isn't all-inclusive but will give you an appreciation for the variety of opportunities that can be pursued by those with accounting degrees.

CFO—The Chief Financial Officer of an entity is typically the most senior financial person working for the organization and is usually a member of the "C-Suite" (senior management team), often serving as a key advisor to the chief executive officer. The CFO possesses significant authority and responsibility and typically is highly compensated. In a publicly held company, the CFO's compensation package usually includes an equity stake in the company in the form of stock options or restricted stock. While they have responsibility for overseeing all accounting and financial reporting functions, CFOs also have broader mandates, including helping raise debt and equity capital, communicating with investors, managing various lender and supplier relationships and myriad other duties. CFOs of publicly traded companies are required to sign "certifications" regarding the accuracy of the periodic financial statements of their companies, which exposes them to legal liability. As a result of their various responsibilities, some CFOs have technical accounting backgrounds, although others have backgrounds in investment banking or finance. Some rise into the role from other levels of management.

Controller—This individual has oversight of the accounting records and maintaining them in accordance with generally accepted accounting principles (GAAP).[16] Also responsible for processes and internal controls related to the accounting and financial reporting functions, controllers typically oversee a team of people that can range from hundreds globally for a large company to just a few people in a start-up or smaller family business.

Director of Financial Reporting—This position tends to exist at larger companies and is responsible for the preparation of financial statements that get distributed to investors and creditors and filed with regulatory agencies, such as the SEC, typically on a quarterly basis.

Accounting Manager—This position oversees a team of accountants and typically reports to the controller.

Treasurer—The treasurer is responsible for handling and managing an organization's cash, investments, and debt obligations. If the organization uses derivative instruments for risk management or hedging purposes, the treasurer would also typically be involved in structuring their use.

Tax Director—This position oversees tax planning and compliance for an organization. In a larger company, the director may be responsible for dozens of staff members and oversees consulting work being done for the company by outside firms.

---

[16] Smaller businesses sometimes do not follow GAAP accounting principles. They may use cash basis accounting or an "other comprehensive basis of accounting."

Director of Internal Audit—Responsible for evaluating compliance with a company's stated policies, procedures, and controls, the internal audit director may oversee a team of staff auditors or supervise work being performed by a third-party firm on an outsourced basis.

Forensic Accountant—Possessing expertise in doing investigations involving potential fraud or non-compliance with laws and regulations, a forensic accountant might work within an internal audit function at a larger company.

Are You an Entrepreneur?

I know many individuals who obtained an accounting degree, worked for a period in public accounting or private industry, and then decided to start their own business. While most of them launched accounting, tax or consulting businesses, a number started businesses that weren't directly related to accounting. For example, one friend and former colleague of mine, Ryan Lafferty, started his own recruiting firm specializing in finding qualified individuals to fill controller vacancies at companies.

Spending a few years working in an accounting role for a firm or in industry can be wonderful training for future entrepreneurs. They get to see first-hand how businesses operate and are financed and learn other important lessons that will help them succeed when they launch their own companies.

Careers in Academia

Individuals who enjoy teaching or research work may desire to pursue a full- or part-time career in the academic world. Below are a few examples of potential roles at colleges and universities.

Tenure-track Professor—This would be a full-time position usually requiring a PhD. Besides earning a salary, a tenure-track professor receives fringe benefits. While expectations can vary by institution, it is usually expected that individuals in this role will do significant research and publish their work in scholarly journals, contributing to the knowledge base of the profession. Many full-time professors are members of the American Accounting Association.[17]

---

[17] See https://aaahq.org for more information.

Non-tenure-track Professor—This could be a full- or part-time-position and may or may not come with fringe benefits such as healthcare coverage and retirement contributions. It typically does not involve research. Teaching loads can be heavy (as much as four classes per semester). An MBA, MS or master's degree in tax is usually required, and most folks in this role also have a form of professional certification, such as a CPA or CMA.

Adjunct Professor—Most universities employ adjuncts to teach one or two classes per semester. Most of these individuals have other full- or part-time jobs and teach in the evenings. Compensation is minimal (perhaps $3,000 to $4,000 per class taught) and usually does not include fringe benefits. There are no research expectations with these roles.

The Bottom Line

Accounting can take you just about anywhere you choose to go, in all types of industries and all sorts of positions. Understand the landscape of opportunities and pursue your passion!

My Own Career Path

Shortly after I became a partner, my firm went to a "line of business" structure, organized by the types of clients or industries we served. Everyone was asked to pick an area of specialization. Most of our professionals joined the "financial services" practice or the "manufacturing, retail and distribution" segment because most of our existing clients operated in those sectors. I chose the "information, communications and entertainment" area, which included clients in the software, telecommunications, semiconductor, and related industries. Many of these clients were emerging-growth companies, often backed by venture capital firms, and that appealed to me. Frankly, I took a bit of a risk because this was somewhat of a new practice area for our office and for me personally.

It turned out to be a great decision. There were only a handful of us in this line of business in our Philadelphia office and I had a chance to work with some remarkably interesting clients. Over the next several years, we had a lot of success in expanding the practice, which I wound up leading. And this positioned me for other opportunities later in my career.

Lesson Learned: Risk can translate into opportunity. But be thoughtful about what risks to accept!

Food for Thought

When my mother took her turn to sit in a gown at graduation, she thought she had only two career options: nursing and teaching. She raised me and my sister to believe that we could do anything, and we believed her.

— Sheryl Sandberg, chief operating officer
of Facebook

CHAPTER FIVE

What About Work–Life Balance?

Key Takeaway

It is possible to experience a successful professional accounting career and achieve your goals while also having a satisfying and rewarding personal and family life.

I worked in public accounting for 36 years and am well familiar with what it takes to be successful, including the extent of overtime that may be required at different times, particularly during the audit or tax busy seasons. With this as context, I am often surprised when I talk with students and others who have never worked in the profession but who somehow "know" that the workloads are extreme.

I'm not sure exactly how this potentially inaccurate picture of the profession is drawn, but I do know that it is sometimes human nature to exaggerate things, and perhaps some practitioners do this in discussing the hours they work. There may be an element of "whisper down the lane" going on as well (i.e., as stories get passed from one person to the next, they get embellished). I fear that sometimes students are getting their information from people who never worked in the profession and have no first-hand basis for their views.

The material in this chapter is based on my experience in public accounting, but I believe my views are also relevant regarding many accounting positions in private industry.

The Reality

Accounting is a seasonal and deadline-driven profession. This translates into periods of extreme demand where overtime is required to complete assignments on a timely basis. That overtime can be significant.

The majority of both public and privately held companies requiring audits use calendar year-ends, meaning that their audited financial statements are presented as of December 31 of each year. Tax return due dates are also based on an entity's year-end. If a company is publicly traded and required to file its financial statements with the Securities and Exchange Commission, the audited statements will be due 60 or 75 or 90 days after the end of their year, depending on the company's size and market capitalization. Most banks and other lenders require audited financials to be provided within similar time frames, although sometimes extended deadlines (e.g., 120 days after year-end) are offered to privately owned companies.

The combination of these factors creates a "busy season" for those working in public accounting audit practices that is particularly demanding from around January 15 through March 15, although the hectic period can extend through April 30. It's not unusual for audit professionals from firms of all sizes to be asked to work 60 to 80 hours a week during this period to get the work done and meet deadlines. Sometimes, the hours can be even longer. Individuals working for companies undergoing audits and trying to produce their year-end financial statements often work overtime during this time of year as well.

Is the busy season the only time of year that auditors will be asked to work overtime? Not necessarily. Quarterly reporting deadlines for public companies can also require overtime. If your client is involved in a merger or acquisition transaction or an initial public offering (IPO) or secondary securities offering where it is attempting to raise capital, extra hours may also be required. Such events tend to occur at any point throughout the year, but it would be unusual for younger professionals, in my experience, to work on more than one or two of these transactions a year.

Are Workload Expectations Different for Tax Professionals?

Tax professionals who spend most of their time doing tax compliance work (i.e., preparation or review of tax returns) also deal with deadlines and busier times of the year (often referred to as "tax season" or "the season"). The most common deadline is April 15, well known to non-accountants because every individual who earns income over a minimum threshold is required to file a federal income tax return by this date. Many tax preparers, particularly in small and midsize accounting firms, work exceptionally long hours in the weeks and months leading up to this date. Although that is the most well-known deadline for tax professionals, there are others. Individual federal income tax returns for high-net-worth individuals, which tend to be more complex, often get "extended." The IRS allows a six-month extension for filing, creating a second "individual tax season deadline" of October 15. Different states also have different due dates for income tax returns. Partnerships and "S Corporations" have a March 15 filing deadline for calendar-year-end entities. So, in summary, tax professionals face various deadlines throughout the year that may require overtime. As with the audit busy season, that overtime can be substantial during these periods.

What if I Work in the Advisory Practice of a Public Accounting Firm?

The good news is that advisory or consulting work is less seasonal. But that doesn't mean that a project you're working on won't have a client-imposed deadline that can require overtime. This makes it hard to predict the times of year that you may be asked to work overtime. Some firms include their merger-and-acquisition (M&A) transaction consulting practices within their advisory groups. The nature of this practice often requires overtime because of a strong sense of urgency to consummate a transaction.

What if I Don't Work for a Public Accounting Firm?

As suggested above, overtime is not uncommon for accountants working in private industry, although it may generally not be as intense as you would experience in public accounting. The amount of overtime you will be expected to work will be very dependent on the facts and circumstances of the entity you work for. For example, is the organization public or private? Is it large or small? Is it well staffed or "lean?" Does the organization have good systems and has it invested in technology that automates certain routine tasks and processes?

Even if you work for an organization that is adequately staffed and has made appropriate investments, it is likely overtime will be required to meet deadlines during the monthly, quarterly or annual closing process. As with public accounting, if your company is raising capital or acquiring another company, extra hours may be required related to those events. Finally, you may be asked to work on or lead a special project that has tight deadlines requiring overtime.

It is worth noting that accounting is not unique when it comes to overtime. Most people working in professions (think law or medicine, for example) don't work "9 to 5" jobs. Having said that, overtime should be reasonable and limited to certain times of year versus an ongoing expectation. Professionally managed organizations with good leaders communicate these expectations effectively and make sure their employees are not "overworked." I'll touch on steps organizations are taking to manage staff workloads in a few paragraphs.

What About Travel?

A certain amount of travel should be expected in public accounting, but the amount will vary greatly based on the size of your firm, the practice you are in and the types of clients you serve.

One benefit of working for a larger firm with many offices is that, in theory, you should travel less because work required at locations outside the city or territory where your office is located could presumably be covered by another, closer office. This is often the case, although sometimes client preferences dictate that out-of-town work be done by the primary engagement team.

It might be helpful to share a bit of my own experience to illustrate this point. I worked in our Philadelphia office. The firm also had offices located in Harrisburg (in central Pennsylvania, about two hours west), Baltimore (about two hours south) and Short Hills, N.J. (about two hours north). We didn't have to worry about markets or clients two hours east of us because that would pretty much put us in the Atlantic Ocean! So, in theory, our clients should generally have been within a 60- to 75-minute trip from Center City Philadelphia. If we went further than that, we were probably entering into our neighboring offices' territory. Given that scenario, overnight travel should have been rare. In most cases, this is how it worked, but there were always exceptions. I had a client whose corporate headquarters was in the Philadelphia suburbs, but that maintained operations and manufacturing facilities at other locations around the country. This client also had a preference that our Philadelphia audit team travel to serve their subsidiaries, even though that company's out-of-pocket expenses would have been lower if the work were done by other, closer offices of our firm.

I also traveled periodically when my clients were involved in acquiring businesses in other geographies.

If you work for a local or regional firm that doesn't have nationwide office locations, but your clients have operations in other geographies, travel may be required more frequently.

From a practice or service-line standpoint, people in the consulting/ advisory side of accounting tend to travel most. I would say the audit practice is next, while the tax practice tends to require less travel (although there are exceptions, depending on the nature of a firm or individual's practice and client base).

Depending on the nature of your clients and whether their operations are global in nature, some of your travel may be international.

Positions at all firms are likely to require a certain amount of non-client-related travel. Early in my career, I typically went out of town for at least a week every year to attend training programs. Later in my career, I was often asked to travel to other cities to attend meetings of my firm's leadership team.

Recognizing that your own experience will be based on specific facts and circumstances that may differ from my experience, it may be helpful to know that I probably averaged about four to five weeks of travel annually during my 36-year career. Everyone is unique and opinions will vary, but I'll conclude this paragraph with two personal observations about travel. The first is that when I was young and single, traveling was fun, especially when I was visiting a city for the first time and had an opportunity to experience it. As my career progressed, travel became more of a chore, especially when I was visiting cities I had been to many times and had more commitments at home.

Regarding jobs outside of public accounting, some travel will probably be required. Again, it will depend on your organization's specific situation but in many cases travel will be less frequent than required in public accounting.

Of course, it is worth noting that the pandemic of 2020–21 resulted in major changes in how people in general accomplish their work and this certainly applies to accountants. Most accountants were able to work remotely during the pandemic, often from the comfort of their own homes. They were frequently able to complete their work effectively without traveling and this is likely to cause firms and companies of all sizes to "rethink" the necessity of travel in the future. No doubt some travel will still be necessary or required but it is quite possible that the amount of travel required by accounting professionals will be less than my personal experience outlined in the preceding paragraphs.

What About Minimum "Chargeable Hour" Quotas?

Accounting firms tend to be particularly good at "measuring stuff." They are also very focused on planning, budgeting and holding people accountable. As a result, most firms set goals for their professionals to generate a certain number of billable hours annually. This number can vary greatly based on the size of the firm, the nature of the practice you are in, your level in the firm and other factors.

In my experience, younger professionals (below manager) will be asked to generate somewhere in the vicinity of 1,800 billable hours a year. When you consider the fact that firms often offer their staff 20 to 25 days of personal time off each year, and that most firms also require a minimum of 40 hours of staff training each year, that doesn't allow for a lot of downtime.

Some Good News About Work–Life Balance

In recent years, accounting firms have been doing a better job of managing the seasonal nature of their businesses. Some techniques that have been effective in this regard include:

✓ Better planning and communication with clients

✓ More interim (before the balance sheet date) work

✓ Improved use of technology

✓ For the larger firms, utilization of offshore resources

I believe there are opportunities for further improvement in how the firms manage their collective resources to meet deadlines. So, while over-time will not go away anytime soon, perhaps circumstances will improve.

In addition, the attitudes of firm leaders have evolved over the years in a positive way. When I started in the profession in the late 1970s, expectations were that "we will do whatever it takes to serve our clients and meet their deadlines, even if that means working around the clock." Today, there is a much greater awareness of work–life balance issues and firms go to great lengths to address them, including providing generous "compensating time off" to employees who work overtime during busy periods.

Many firms also offer compensated "shutdown" periods around the holidays in December or during the summer around the Fourth of July.

Let me share a few tips, techniques and strategies designed to minimize unnecessary overtime hours (for both you, and, as your career progresses, your teams):

✓ Plan effectively

✓ Be (and stay) organized

✓ Prioritize

✓ Communicate

✓ Delegate

✓ Use technology effectively (including working remotely, when appropriate)

✓ Learn how to say no (don't be your own worst enemy by taking on too much)

Effectively Using Your Time Off

As mentioned earlier in this chapter, compensated time off can be the equivalent of 4 to 5 weeks of paid vacation a year at many employers. The good news is: That's a lot of time off! The bad news: It can sometimes be challenging to find the right times (that work both for you and your employer) to use it. Unfortunately, some organizations have a "use it or lose it" policy, and I have seen more than a few young professionals wind up not fully taking advantage of this benefit.

The key is good (and proactive) planning. Understand your employer's policies and develop a plan early in the year as to how to effectively use your days off so that you both comply with policies and meet your needs. Don't wait until you're deep into the year to think about it, as procrastination could result in a problematic situation for either your or your employer.

One More Tip!

A good friend of mine shared some helpful advice he heard early in his career about work–life balance. Sometimes, it can be hard to achieve in the short term and it is not realistic to think that every day, week or month will be perfectly balanced. There are going to be periods of time where you are putting in extra hours at work due to deadlines or the demands of your career. There will also be times when your family and personal life will require more time and attention, for instance, if you have a parent or relative dealing with a heath-care crisis and you need to be there for them. The most important thing is to be able to achieve balance over the long term, that is, to be able to prioritize and devote attention to your most significant professional and personal priorities when necessary and appropriate.

How I Balanced Personal Priorities and a Busy Workload

My son was a baseball player and I coached him from the time he was 7 until he turned 17. These were some of the busiest and most demanding years of my career. Our weeknight games would usually start at 5. As the head coach, I needed to be there an hour before game time for batting practice, infield drills, etc. Depending on where we were playing, I might need to leave by mid-afternoon to make a game on time. I would treat these commitments like important client meetings. They would go on my calendar and I would stick to them. That is because I made them a priority. Often, I would work extra hours the day before or after a game to compensate for "leaving early." But I rarely missed a game, and I never missed a client deadline.

Lesson Learned: Make sure your priorities reflect your values and allocate your time accordingly.

Food for Thought

We think, mistakenly, that success is the result of the amount of time we put in at work, instead of the quality of time put in.

—Arianna Huffington, author and businesswoman

CHAPTER SIX

The Profession's Diversity, Equity and Inclusion Journey

Key Takeaway

There has never been a better time for women, people of color and other underrepresented groups to pursue a career in the accounting profession.

The bad news for women and members of racial or ethnic minorities considering careers in accounting is that the profession has not historically been a leader in creating opportunities and career paths for them. As a result, there are not as many partners, CFOs, and professionals in leadership roles from these demographic groups as there should be. The good news is that the profession is painfully aware of its less-than-stellar performance in this area and has made strides in recent years in addressing the issue. This is particularly true of the largest firms, all of which have publicly embraced a commitment to diversity and inclusion as a top strategic priority. As a result, I believe there has never been a better time for a woman or an ethnic minority to be entering the profession.

Recruitment and Retention

For decades, the profession has recruited men and women in largely equal numbers. Unfortunately, there was not as much focus on retention programs. Often, women who were good at what they did, but wanted to start a family, would leave when that time came with little or no discussion by their employers of flex programs, sabbaticals, or part-time arrangements. In recent years, this has changed. Firms have come to the realization that they spend a significant amount of time, effort and money in identifying, onboarding and training talent and that it is shortsighted to let qualified people with long-term potential depart just because they want to have a family. Firms are much more open to the prospect of employees taking time off to have or adopt a child and then returning to work on a part-time basis. Many firms have special programs designed to address these circumstances and some have been quite successful in making them work. As a result, the rate of retention of women at the manager and partner levels in public accounting firms has increased considerably in recent years.

Regarding racial and ethnic minorities, the track record on recruitment has not been as strong in the past, but this also has changed over the last decade or so. Today, firms are eager to hire qualified ethnic minorities, and many have special programs designed to identify and attract such men and women. The large firms are also striving to retain this talent, although their track record on retaining minority employees is not as good as it is with women. Nonetheless, the growing awareness of this challenge has led to significantly increased emphasis over the last decade. Many firms are focusing more time, energy and resources on addressing it. Still, more work needs to be done here. Research by my friend and former colleague Frank Ross, who runs the Center for Accounting Education at Howard University, indicates that accounting firms and other employers can do a better job of making ethnic minorities feel welcome in their work environments.[18]

Affinity Groups

Many large accounting firms and corporate employers have established "affinity groups" where individuals with common backgrounds and similar challenges and opportunities can develop relationships that will help them succeed, professionally and personally. For example, "women's professional networks" often exist in large organizations, catering to female

---

[18] Day, M.; Lim, L.; Little, C., Ross, F. (2019). "Challenges Continue for African-American Accountants." *Journal of Accountancy*, 19 January.

professionals from the entry level to senior management roles. The groups' events and programming can be either professionally or personally themed, but the common denominator is a forum where women professionals can come together, network and build relationships with the help and support of their employers. Mentoring relationships often develop through these networks, which can be instrumental in helping employees succeed and— a big plus for the employer—improve retention rates. Similar groups exist for minority group members in many organizations.

At KPMG's Philadelphia office, the firm had an African American network, a Hispanic network, and an Asian network, to name a few, in addition to our network for women. We also had groups for LGBTQ professionals and military veterans. While the programming can vary to reflect the interests and focus of these respective groups, the sense of community and belonging they facilitate is consistent.

Affinity groups (now referred to as "Business Resource Groups" by at least one Big Four firm) like these largely did not exist 15 years ago. The fact that they have developed and prospered bodes well for the future. While not a cure-all, affinity groups should help with retention.

Affinity groups have been an important step in the profession's journey toward diversity, equality and inclusion (DEI) but, to its credit, the profession continues to evolve and elevate its focus on being a leader in these important areas. Recently, several Big Four firms and at least one second-tier firm have published reports on their progress, strategy and initiatives relative to DEI matters. Areas of focus in the reports include:

✓ Details of the demographic composition of current workforce by gender and ethnicity

✓ Target objectives regarding how workforce demographics will change in the coming years

✓ Information on the gender and ethnicity of recent recruits

✓ Trends in demographic information

✓ Breakdown of recent promotions from a gender and ethnicity perspective

✓ Details of initiatives and programs the firms have launched to enhance workplace diversity

✓ Information regarding supplier diversity programs

✓ Statements of leadership commitment and support

These reports reflect a level of transparency and commitment to improving the DEI situation at the firms as well as a willingness to be held accountable in a data-driven manner, which is encouraging!

Leadership Programs

Many organizations have also rolled out leadership training programs for underrepresented minorities in the last decade or so. These programs are intended to encourage, motivate, and develop high-potential employees. While most firms and companies have had leadership training programs for decades, the focus on programs designed specifically for women and ethnic minorities is a relatively recent development.

At KPMG in Philadelphia, we launched a Women's Leadership Training program to address these issues. It was a year-long program, facilitated by a professional training firm and including women from our firm as well as from other leading Philadelphia-area companies. The program proved to be so successful it was eventually emulated by many other KPMG offices and continues to this day.

The AICPA has a leadership program for aspiring accountants who are underrepresented minorities and are considering a "CPA path." Most participants are college and university students majoring in accounting who have demonstrated high potential. Over three days, they get to hear from leaders in the profession about their own career journeys and why accounting is a great profession to pursue. In recent years, about 100 students a year have participated in the AICPA's "Accounting Scholars Leadership Workshop."

Certain state CPA societies and firms of all sizes offer similar recognition and leadership development programs. Such programs can have a significant impact in motivating individuals to stay with their employers or in the profession.

The PhD Project

Established in 1994, the PhD Project was founded upon the premise that advancements in workplace diversity could be propelled by increasing the diversity of business school faculty. The program strives to assist Black/African American, Latinx/Hispanic American and Native Americans attain their business PhD and become the business professors who will mentor the next generation of leaders.

The project has been very successful with over 1,200 minority business professors having earned their doctoral degrees with its support. As a result, many students have benefited from the knowledge mentoring, guidance and perspective of these professors.

While the PhD project is not focused exclusively on the accounting profession, many of its participants are accounting professors and this important strategic initiative has received considerable funding and support from the profession over the years, a demonstration of the commitment to a more diverse, inclusive, and equitable profession.

Leadership Roles

Several organizations have become much more proactive in considering women and ethnic minorities for senior leadership roles. Some even follow the "Rooney Rule"[19] that requires that a woman or minority be considered whenever a leadership post is being filled. Employers may also have a protocol that requires that someone who is considered but not selected for the leadership role be provided with coaching and feedback to help address the development needs that caused them to fall short. The goal is to help the candidate be better prepared to succeed when the next opening occurs.

---

[19] Named for Dan Rooney, former owner of the Pittsburgh Steelers and chairman of the National Football League's diversity committee.

Programs like this are important because women and minorities in leadership roles can serve as powerful role models for younger professionals the firm is striving to retain. For far too many years, women and minorities did not see role models at the highest levels of their firms or companies. This is starting to change (two of the Big Four firms have recently had a woman as their chief executive officer) but is very much a work in process, with much more that needs to be done. The encouraging news is that each of the Big Four firms has seen a steady increase in the percentage of its partners who are women or ethnic minorities. More progress in this area is needed at firms of all sizes.

Tips for Success

In addition to the general advice that I've offered throughout this book, here are some specific thoughts and suggestions for women and ethnic minorities pursuing professional accounting careers:

✓ **Find a sponsor**—A sponsor is invested in your career success and has influence; they are different than a mentor in that they can advocate for you in a way that makes a difference.[20]

✓ **Identify role models**—If there is no one at a senior level within your organization, find someone outside your organization who is willing to help (you may be surprised at how many successful people are willing to help if you ask).

---

[20] Mobley, K. (2019). "Understanding the Impact of Mentorship versus Sponsorship." *Forbes*, 17 September.

✓ **Seek high-profile assignments**—Take on tasks or challenges that provide an opportunity to showcase your potential.

✓ **Get involved**—If your organization hasn't done a good job of retaining talent, become part of the solution by volunteering to mentor and coach younger colleagues.

✓ **Share your ideas**—Offer suggestions to leaders at your organization about how to improve the situation.

What I Learned by Being a Mentor

I had the opportunity to mentor both women and ethnic minorities during my career. I came to understand that they faced unique challenges that required unique solutions. I also learned that in professional services (and just about every other business), "talent wins" and that talent comes in many different forms. Organizations that aren't accessing 100% of the talent pool (including women and minorities) will eventually lose to those that are doing so.

Lesson Learned: Make a real effort to be aware of your own "unconscious biases" (we all have them) and strive to be an ally for colleagues from underrepresented groups.

Food for Thought

Women and girls can do whatever they want. There is no limit to what we as women can accomplish.

— Michelle Obama, former First Lady of the United States

Section Two

Growing in Your Early Career Years by Mastering Important Fundamentals

CHAPTER SEVEN

Core Values Every Accountant Should Embrace

 Key Takeaway

Certain core values are essential to your success as a professional accountant. It is critically important to understand this and commit to embracing behaviors that will build trust, credibility and respect.

Accounting is a profession, just like law or medicine. Let's look at what that means by reviewing the six characteristics of a profession[21] summarized below:

- ✓ Renders a specialized service based upon advanced knowledge and skills.
- ✓ Involves a confidential relationship between a practitioner and a client or an employer.
- ✓ Is charged with a substantial degree of public obligation.
- ✓ Requires a common body of knowledge to be mastered by acquiring and demonstrating specific skills.
- ✓ Serves the public interest.
- ✓ Is bound by a code of ethics governing its relationships with clients, colleagues and the public.

Successful accountants recognize their status as members of a profession and embrace the responsibilities that come with that status. But what does it really mean to be a professional? Here is how the dictionary defines

---

[21] W.E. Wickenden.

a professional (my source for this and the definitions that follow in this chapter was the *Merriam-Webster Dictionary*):

Professional—*Engaged in one of the learned professions; characterized or conforming to technical or ethical standards of a profession; exhibiting a courteous, conscientious, and generally businesslike manner in the workplace.*

In a formal sense, being a professional means meeting minimum educational requirements and demonstrating appropriate knowledge and expertise in your field. If you choose to serve the public by providing "attest" services (for example, if you are an auditor working in "public accounting"), it means passing an exam and obtaining a license. It also involves complying with the profession's code of conduct and committing to continuous learning (i.e., staying current in your field).

In a less formal but very practical way, being a professional means acting like one. This entails dressing appropriately for your environment, showing up on time and taking your work seriously or "exercising due professional care."

Accounting professionals are held to a high standard of conduct and for good reason: ***The public relies on their work!*** Investors, creditors, regulators and other third parties depend on accountants to do the right thing and do it in a professional fashion. A failure to embrace these high standards and keep the public interest in mind can have disastrous results. When Enron failed in 2002, its collapse was triggered, in part, by an accounting scandal. As a result, thousands of Enron employees lost their jobs and the company's investors suffered significant losses. Ultimately, Enron's auditing firm also failed, creating major disruption in capital markets not only in the United States but globally as well.

Being professional in your actions and mindset builds trust. Failing to do so destroys trust. In business, trust is like oxygen. It is essential.

Let's review the definition of trust, according to the dictionary:

Trust—*Assured reliance on the character, ability, strength or truth of someone or something; one in which confidence is placed; dependence on something future or contingent (hope); a charge or duty imposed in faith or confidence or as a condition of some relationship; something committed or entrusted to one to be used or cared for in the interest of another. Synonyms include confidence, credence, faith, stock.*

Notice the power and import of the words used to define the concept of trust: character, strength, truth, confidence, dependence, and faith. These are not just words; they are important values that every accountant should embrace. The efficient functioning of our capital markets system in the United States (arguably the best in the world) depends heavily on accountants honoring the trust that has been placed in them by doing the right thing. A robust and reliable capital markets system serves as the underpinning of a strong economy that supports hundreds of millions of American citizens.

Trust, of course, is earned. One of the best ways to build trust with others is to simply do what you say you are going to do, on both a timely and consistent basis. Trust is also established and reinforced when individuals consistently act with Integrity. Again, let's look at the dictionary definition of that term:

Integrity—*Firm adherence to a code of especially moral or artistic values; an unimpaired condition; the quality or state of being complete or undivided. Synonyms include character, decency, goodness, honesty, morality, probity, rectitude, righteousness, rightness, uprightness, virtue, and virtuousness.*

Again, this definition and its synonyms incorporate some inspiring words and concepts. And they suggest a commitment to doing the right thing by following a code of moral values. Interestingly, over the years, the accounting profession has developed a formal written code of conduct to help address potential conflicts of interest and assist professionals dealing with ethical issues. A fundamental step in your commitment to be a successful accountant is to embrace high ethical standards.

Let's review the dictionary definition of ethics:

Ethics—*A set of moral principles; a theory or system of moral values; the principles of conduct governing an individual or group; a guiding philosophy; a consciousness of moral importance. Synonyms include morality, norms, principles, and standards.*

I never cease to be amazed at how common ethical lapses are, not just in the business world but in virtually every field, including the worlds of sports, politics, and entertainment, to name just a few. It is hard to observe the daily news and not see at least one alleged incident of fraud or other criminal behavior. The following are only some of the headlines about ethical lapses that appeared as I was writing this book:

✓ **College admissions bribery scandal**—Federal prosecutors brought charges against more than 50 individuals, including prominent names from the worlds of business, entertainment, and sports, alleging that they had engaged in crimes—including bribery and money laundering—to help their children gain admission to top colleges and universities. Many of those charged have been convicted and served prison time.

✓ **United Auto Workers corruption matter**—More than ten officials of the UAW, one of the largest and most prestigious unions in the world, were charged with embezzlement and other crimes that victimized the union's membership. Several defendants were convicted and jailed.

✓ **Aircraft safety shortcuts**—Boeing, one of America's largest companies, agreed to pay $2.5 billion to resolve a U.S. Justice Department investigation. Boeing admitted that employees misled aviation regulators about safety issues linked to two deadly crashes of its 737 MAX airliner.

✓ **Political corruption**—Duncan Hunter, who represented California's 50th Congressional District from 2013 to 2020, and his wife were indicted on multiple counts of wire fraud, falsifying records, violating campaign finance laws, and conspiracy. The couple was accused of conspiring to misuse $250,000 in campaign funds for personal expenses and of filing false campaign finance reports. Both were convicted, and the former congressman was sentenced to eleven months in prison.

✓ **Cheating in sports**—The Houston Astros baseball team inappropriately used technology to steal signs during the 2017 and 2018 seasons (a video camera was used to pick up signals from the opposing catcher, and the signs were relayed to Astros hitters). As a result, the Astros' general manager and field manager were suspended for the 2020 season. The team also was fined $5 million and forfeited first- and second-round selections in the 2020 and 2021 player drafts. The scandal also resulted in lawsuits against the Astros and Major League Baseball.

While people in every field need to be aware and alert to the risk of ethical lapses, poor decisions and inappropriate behavior, accountants, by virtue of their chosen profession, are held to a particularly high standard in this regard.

Of course, avoiding ethical lapses can require courage. How does the dictionary define courage?

Courage—*Mental or moral strength to venture, persevere and withstand danger, fear, or difficulty. Synonyms include bravery, daring, dauntlessness, fearlessness, guts, heart, heroism, intestinal fortitude, moxie, nerve, valor and virtue.*

You may be surprised that I believe courage is an important trait for an accountant to possess and demonstrate. But my view is based on many personal experiences during a career that spanned four decades. You will find, unfortunately, that people are sometimes particularly good at rationalizing why their position is correct or acceptable when in fact it is not. Such a scenario requires the accountant to ask the hard questions and sometimes "speak truth to power."

Losing a Client to Protect Our Integrity

Early in my career, I was the manager on an audit of a client in the construction industry that owned two hotel properties that were highly leveraged, or indebted. The accounting rules for many years had a provision that permitted the non-consolidation of certain subsidiaries operating in a different industry than a company's primary industry. Historically, these rules applied to my client. By not consolidating the highly indebted hotel subsidiaries in its financial statements, thus keeping a significant amount of debt off the balance sheet, the company made its financial position look stronger than it really was.

The Financial Accounting Standards Board (FASB) eventually changed these rules in a way that required consolidation of all majority-owned subsidiaries, regardless of the industry they were in. We advised the client that it would need to consolidate the hotels. The company's leaders were unwilling to do this because they were concerned the company's financial statements would be viewed negatively due to the additional debt. After many contentious discussions, the company advised us that it was going to change auditors unless we reversed our position. We refused to do so, and the company made a change in accountants. While it was unfortunate to lose a client, this was a powerful lesson for me about doing the right thing, even when it hurt my firm in the short term. My firm recognized its responsibility to the third-party investors and creditors who would be relying on those audited financial statements to make important business decisions and was unwilling to sacrifice its integrity for the sake of retaining a client.

Lesson Learned: Always do the right thing, even when the short-term consequences may be painful.

Food for Thought

Be more concerned with your character than your reputation, because your character is what you really are, while your reputation is merely what others think you are.

—John Wooden, former UCLA men's basketball coach, whose teams won 10 NCAA national championships

CHAPTER EIGHT

Developing and Enhancing Your Technical Skills

Key Takeaway

Your technical skills are the currency that will finance your professional career. Commit to constantly developing and enhancing them and adopt a philosophy of continuous life-long learning and improvement.

Your technical skills as an accountant are essential to your success. They are what makes you valuable to an employer, whether you work for a company, an accounting firm, or a nonprofit organization. You possess specialized training and knowledge that your employer needs to run its business.

While the fundamentals of accounting are learned by earning a college or university degree in the field, that is merely the beginning of your journey, sort of like table stakes in a poker game. You have both the responsibility and opportunity to continue learning and growing throughout your career. While this is an important concept to embrace for anyone entering the workforce, it is particularly critical for accountants because accounting and tax rules are constantly changing. Committing to a philosophy and mindset of continuous learning and investing in your future will serve you well and pay dividends throughout your career. This chapter includes a variety of tips and suggestions that are focused on helping you strengthen and enhance your technical skills on a sustained basis.

The Importance of Reading and Staying Current

Sometimes I think reading is becoming a lost art, particularly when I interact with today's college-aged students.[22] I understand that technology has altered cultural norms and that students today get most of their news and information via their mobile devices. There is nothing wrong with this. I do, however, think it is important to get beyond the headlines that, along with snippets of opinion and information (but, often, not a lot of analysis), tend to dominate social media sites. Regardless of whether your source for news and information is digital or print, try to obtain your information from sources that are credible, unbiased and objective.

I encourage students I meet with to try to spend time every day reading the *Wall Street Journal* or other business publications. Student subscriptions to business publications can often be obtained at a discount and are available electronically. The AICPA and other organizations offer daily alerts and newsletters designed to keep readers current on important developments in the profession. Being current and knowledgeable about the business and broader world can be a huge contributor to your success. As your career progresses, staying abreast of developments in your field or area of expertise becomes even more important. Make sure you take advantage of technical alerts and other notifications issued internally by your firm or company. By the way, if you are not convinced about the importance of reading to your success, consider this information about some names you will recognize:[23]

- ✓ Bill Gates reads about 50 books per year

- ✓ Mark Cuban reads more than three hours every day

- ✓ Oprah Winfrey called reading "the strongest signal for success in the future that I've ever seen."[24]

- ✓ Elon Musk is an avid reader. When asked how he learned to build rockets, he said "I read books."

- ✓ Mark Zuckerberg resolved to read a book every two weeks throughout 2015.

---

[22] Gioia, D. (November 2007). "To Read or Not to Read, a Question of National Consequence." *Research Report #47, National Endowment for the Arts.* 5–22.

[23] Quartz Ideas (www.qz.com).

[24] Winfrey, O. (2015). "Oprah on the Key to Success." *Oprah.com* (21 July). Video 2:13. www.oprah.com/own-oprahshow/oprah-on-the-key-to-success-video

Jamie Dimon, the CEO of JPMorgan Chase, is also an avid reader and recommends it to others. In an interview with LinkedIn, in response to a question about career advice for young people, he said: "I read four or five newspapers every morning. I read tons of stuff."[25]

Learning from Others

On the job training (OTJT) is a great vehicle to develop your technical skills, particularly early in your career. To maximize the benefits of OTJT, get in the habit of asking lots of questions. I'm a firm believer in the adage, "There is no such thing as a stupid question" (other than the one that does not get asked). Of course, a reasonable effort to study and analyze a situation by yourself should precede your questions. This approach will help you learn certain things independently and ensure that the questions you do direct to your colleagues or supervisor are well thought out and demonstrate the effort you've expended on the topic.

You can also learn a lot by observing more experienced professionals in action. Or, as Yogi Berra, the famous baseball player and manager, supposedly put it: "You can observe a lot by just watching."

What do your colleagues do well? Why are they successful? What traits of theirs warrant emulation? By the way, you can also learn by observing things people do *not* do so well (i.e., what *not* to do).

Training and Professional Development Programs: An Overlooked Fringe Benefit

When considering accepting a position with a new employer, whether it's your first job or a transition situation, most people critically evaluate the proposed compensation and benefits such as health insurance, retirement plans, paid time off (holidays, vacation, etc.) and a variety of other factors. This is entirely appropriate, of course. However, in my experience, many people don't consider one of the most important benefits offered by prospective employers: their training programs. This factor is critically

---

[25] "Jamie Dimon on how to be successful," December 18, 2018, interview with Daniel Roth, Editor in Chief of LinkedIn (available at https://www.lynda.com).

important in a knowledge-based economy where the pace of change has never been greater and your ability to continue to learn new things will be integral to your future success. And, in my experience, there can be a wide disparity in the quality, breadth and depth of employer training programs. Top-notch organizations have a commitment to continuous learning and make it a priority to invest in learning and development programs for their people. Be sure to understand a prospective employer's level of investment in your future learning and development. It may be the most important benefit it offers you!

Specialized Knowledge (Becoming an Expert)

Developing unique knowledge and expertise in a subject area can be a great way to advance your career. When you become the most knowledgeable individual about a topic at your company or firm, others will seek you out to tap into your expertise. This will create more exposure for you and often lead to advancement opportunities. There are many areas where experts are needed. By way of example, here are a few: data and analytics (auditing), derivative instruments (accounting), international taxation (tax) and helping install an SAP system (consulting). It's hard for everyone at a firm or company to be an expert in everything, so developing deep subject-matter expertise in a particular area can result in you being more valuable to your colleagues and employer. Such specialized knowledge can typically also be easily translated across organizations and even across industries.

I believe a great time in your career to begin to develop specialized knowledge and expertise is after about three to four years of experience but before you've reached ten years of experience. If you start too soon, you may not have a chance to understand and evaluate the variety of options. Conversely, if you wait too long, you'll fall behind others who began to focus sooner. Your ability to develop specialized expertise will come from both your work experience and the specific technical training you obtain.

Specialized Industry Knowledge

When I began my career, exposure to many different industries and clients (large and small, public and private companies, etc.) was considered a good thing. During the first three years of my public accounting career, I worked on audits or other engagements involving: a publicly held manufacturing company listed on the New York Stock Exchange; a county government; a privately owned construction company; a savings and loan institution; a shipping company; a school district; a university, and an automobile dealership, to name a few. Each organization had a different accounting system and I dealt with a variety of personalities. The learning curve was phenomenal, and I believe I benefited from being exposed to so many different types of organizations. Eventually, I specialized in serving technology-oriented emerging growth companies.

As the business world has grown more complex, many firms, especially larger ones, endeavor to have their professionals develop an industry specialization and focus early on in their careers. There is a difference between being a subject-matter expert and an industry expert. The latter has a deep understanding of the business model and issues unique to a particular segment of the economy (e.g., oil and gas, airlines, pharmaceuticals, banking, etc.).

Whether you begin to specialize earlier or later in your career, know that it can become a competitive advantage. Industry knowledge and expertise strengthens your personal balance sheet by expanding and deepening your technical skills. Many industries follow specialized accounting, tax, and reporting principles that you will need to master to advance at a company in those industries or an accounting firm that serves clients in those industries.

Sharing Your Knowledge

As your career progresses, you'll have opportunities to teach and develop others. As a manager, I was asked to lead technical presentations given to my colleagues on various accounting and auditing topics. I also had the opportunity to serve as an instructor at the firm's national training programs. I found these situations were great opportunities to strengthen my technical skills. Preparing for these presentations sharpened my knowledge of the topic I was teaching and, inevitably, questions raised by the participants would also help round out my knowledge and expertise in the subject matter.

As my career progressed, I was asked to serve as a speaker or panelist to groups outside the firm in a variety of forums. I also had the chance to write articles for technical publications. These situations were also great learning experiences that enhanced and further developed my technical skills. Make sure you take advantage of these opportunities when you have the chance!

Sharing your knowledge also provides great opportunities for networking, developing your "brand" and establishing credibility inside and outside your organization.

Performing High-quality Work

Obtaining and maintaining technical knowledge and expertise is essential, but the fashion in which you use your skills may be even more important to your long-term success. Applying "due professional care" is critically important. The concept is defined as follows:

"Every person who offers his or her services to another and is employed assumes the duty to exercise in the employment such skill as he or she possesses with reasonable care and diligence. In all of these employments where peculiar skill is requisite, if one offers their services, they are understood as holding themselves out to the public as holding the degree of skill commonly possessed by others in the same employment, and if his pretensions are unfounded, he commits a species of fraud upon everyone who employs him in reliance on his public profession. But no person, whether skilled or unskilled, undertakes that the task they assume shall be performed successfully, and without fault or error; he undertakes for good faith and integrity, but not for infallibility, and he is liable to his employer for negligence, bad faith or dishonesty but not for losses consequent on pure errors of judgment."[26]

In other words, as professionals we have a responsibility to only take on tasks we are qualified to perform and to do our best to do the finest job we can under the circumstances!

---

[26] Cooley on Torts, 1878, referred to by the AICPA in "Audit and Attest Standards."

How I Tried to Learn from Colleagues

In the formative years of my career, I was fortunate to work for many different individuals at my firm. I noticed that each person had strengths and weaknesses. Some were outstanding technically. Others were good at analyzing and solving difficult problems or excelled in managing client relationships. On the weakness side, some were not well organized, others tended to take shortcuts, and a few did not communicate well. I resolved to not worry about their weaknesses but to closely study each person's strengths and learn as much as I could from each of them in the areas where they excelled. This approach served me very well as I learned a lot of different skills from them that I believe made me a much more versatile and well-rounded professional.

Lesson Learned: Pick up as much as you can from more experienced colleagues.

Food for Thought

The best investment you can make is in yourself.

— Warren Buffett, famous investor, CEO of Berkshire Hathaway

CHAPTER NINE

Working Effectively with Others

Key Takeaway

Your ability to work collaboratively and effectively with other people will have a significant impact on your long-term career success.

I suppose a good argument can be made that the ability to work effectively with others is important in just about any profession or occupation. Having said that, I would argue it is particularly important in the accounting profession. Let's look at a few typical scenarios:

✓ **Public Accounting**—You are an auditor and, to do your job well, you need to obtain and review certain information supporting the client's financial statements and significant transactions. After you complete your initial review, you'll need to discuss and resolve any questions or concerns with the appropriate client personnel. You will interact with a variety of individuals in the process of obtaining and auditing that information. Each has a "day job" and other priorities to deal with besides your audit work. Your ability to obtain their cooperation and work effectively with them will be critically important to completing your work in a timely, efficient and effective manner.

✓ **Private Accounting**—You are the accounting manager responsible for closing the books. You have four or five people who are involved in the process reporting directly to you and there are several other departments (e.g., information technology) and an external vendor (payroll processor) that supply information your team needs for the closing process. Your ability to collaborate productively with all these constituencies is essential to meeting your deadlines and compiling accurate financial statements.

✓ **Business Owner**—You operate your own firm which specializes in preparing tax returns for small businesses. To prepare those returns accurately, you need quite a bit of information from your clients and need to ask them certain questions. Some of your clients don't have sophisticated accounting systems and sometimes all the information you require is not available when initial documents are submitted, requiring follow-up calls or emails with your clients. Sometimes, clients may be hesitant to share what they perceive to be "sensitive" or "confidential" information. However, without this information, you're unable to prepare accurate tax returns. Your ability to build trust with clients will be vital in serving them well.

If you take these three scenarios and factor in some "real world" dynamics, such as the people you are dealing with may be under pressure, are perhaps distracted by personal matters or are simply difficult to interact with from a personality standpoint, you'll begin to appreciate the importance to an accountant's success of being able to work effectively with people.

As a general rule, being professional, courteous, and respectful in your dealings with others is a good platform for success. However, there are additional specific skills and strategies that will help. Here are a few to think about and strive to master:

Planning—Being organized and identifying the documents and information you will be needing from others well in advance can go a long way in promoting effective interactions. People appreciate advance notice. Everyone is busy and the more notice you can provide, the better. If you supply someone with a "request list" a month in advance, things will go much better than if they get it a day in advance.

Communications—Putting together a request list is great, but does the person receiving it really understand why you're asking for these items and the reason they are important? Make the time to reach out and talk through it with them. Resolving questions or potential misunderstandings early in the process will go a long way toward heading off issues, delays or the "blame game" down the line.

Listening—Are you an active listener (versus focusing on what you are going to say after the other person stops talking)? Many people are not. Being a good listener can be an invaluable trait in facilitating strong relationships and building trust. Summarizing the takeaways from a conversation is a simple but effective way to make sure you and another person are on the same page.

Empathy—It can be particularly helpful to try to see a situation from the perspective of the other person and appreciate the constraints and challenges they may be wrestling with. Some people tend to take an "it's not my problem" approach to what others are dealing with. But when your success depends upon cooperation and assistance from others, their problem can quickly become your problem. Taking a few minutes to understand and relate to someone else's challenges is usually very much appreciated by the other person and can sometimes be a great learning experience for you, too. It also builds trust and strengthens relationships.

Establishing Checkpoints—In the examples covered above, completing the tasks involved could take from a few days to a few weeks to a few months or longer. Monitoring progress toward completion, identifying open items or matters requiring follow-up and providing timely feedback are all examples of good project management. These periodic check-ins are an effective way to avoid misunderstandings and bad feelings and keep things moving. Those you're dealing with will appreciate you staying in touch!

Ideally, using these techniques will minimize the number of challenging situations you encounter. But I've found that it is somewhat inevitable that you'll be placed in situations where you need to have a difficult conversation with the person you're dealing with. Here are examples of some circumstances I experienced during my career that required having a difficult conversation:

✓ Delivering news that a client doesn't want to hear (For example: "We are going to propose a major adjustment to your financial statements that could materially decrease the earnings your company reports.")

✓ Having to tell someone that their expectations are unreasonable.

✓ Having to tell someone they were not getting a promotion they were expecting.

Here are some tips for having those difficult conversations:

✓ Be honest and respectful

✓ Be factual

✓ Be direct (don't beat around the bush)

✓ Be empathetic but,

✓ Be firm

Do Not Be Intimidated

Some people will try to steamroll you. They will accuse you of not being prepared, asking a foolish question or not being knowledgeable about their business. Stand your ground. Be polite, be professional but be persistent. As I gained more experience, I noticed that people who took this approach often were trying to distract me because they had something they didn't want me to know.

Treat People Consistently

Strive to be polite, courteous, and respectful to everyone you deal with. Their rank in the organization should not matter. Some individuals I know would treat senior individuals in a company much better than they would treat the people at the bottom of the organizational chart. I recommend that you try to build the same relationship and rapport with the most junior employees of a company as you do with an organization's CEO.

One last tip about working with people. When I was interacting with someone, whether it was a colleague of mine or a client, I tried to get to know a little bit about that individual on a personal level. Were they married? Did they have kids? What sports or other activities did they enjoy in their spare time? Inevitably, I found some "common ground" with most people. This type of personal connection can be extremely helpful in developing a relationship and building rapport with people.

A Concluding Thought

Be nice to people you encounter along your career journey and treat them the way you would like to be treated. As a practical matter, the world is a small place, and your paths may cross again. More important, it's the right thing to do.

An Early Lesson in the Value of Listening

On one of my first assignments as an audit manager, I learned early in the engagement that a client official we dealt extensively with was not too happy with our firm and that this individual was also extremely difficult for our people to deal with. They perceived him as hostile and unreasonable. I must admit that I shared that view, based on my initial exposure to this fellow and the way he treated me. However, I invited him to meet me for coffee offsite to get to know him better and to understand his concerns. Over time, we developed a relationship, and I came to understand his thought process and the basis for his views. While some of his complaints were a result of a misunderstanding of our role as the independent auditor, he had other issues that were quite legitimate and warranted some changes in our approach to serving the client. I learned a lot about the importance of listening, empathy, and good communication skills from this individual. When I made partner a few years later, one of the first people to call to congratulate me was this gentleman.

Lesson Learned: Make the time to listen to others and understand their concerns.

Food for Thought

The most important single ingredient in the formula of success is knowing how to get along with people.

—Theodore Roosevelt, 26th president of
  the United States

CHAPTER TEN

Developing Your Communication Skills

Key Takeaway

Successful accountants need to be able to communicate well, both when speaking and in writing. Invest the time to develop your communication skills!

How effectively do you communicate? I ask this question because during my career I encountered many accountants who were very bright, hard-working, and technically proficient but who never achieved their full potential because they were not particularly good communicators. Well-developed communication skills are important in achieving your career growth objectives and a lack of these skills can be a limiting factor in career advancement.

It's especially important for accountants to be able to effectively communicate the results of their work: findings, conclusions, recommendations, etc. In fact, one criticism I occasionally hear about the core assurance and tax services provided by the profession is that they are "commodities," implying that there is little or no difference between the audit report or signature on a tax return of one firm or practitioner compared to another. A great way to address this concern is being able to effectively communicate the results of your work by sharing observations, insights and suggestions with the individuals who engaged you (or those you work for). This will both differentiate you from others and demonstrate your value. To do this effectively requires both an awareness that it is important and the ability to share your feedback in a coherent, articulate, and logical fashion. Some accountants don't realize this should be a priority until later in their careers. Therefore, they lose years of opportunity to enhance their communication skills and make their contributions more valuable to their clients or employer.

Myth—Good Communication Skills Are Related to Personality and Good Communicators Are Amiable and Enjoy "Talking With People."

This is *not* necessarily the case. I've worked with and observed many excellent communicators who were not outgoing by nature.

There are many ways to communicate: through informal conversations, in writing and via formal presentations, to name a few. We'll explore each of these in this chapter but one overriding theme that governs all forms of good communication is to be thoughtful and intentional about *what* you're trying to convey, and clear on why the message is important to the recipient.

The Importance of Effective Writing

Many people, and even some in the profession, still think accountants need only to be "good with numbers." While it certainly doesn't hurt to have strong mathematical skills, I believe it is even more important to be able to write effectively, particularly in an era when computers are so powerful and can do much of the "numbers-crunching." Much of the work accountants perform has to be documented in formal work papers. Sometimes documentation takes the form of memoranda or other written communications that summarize processes, controls, accounting issues, tax positions, findings, recommendations, and many other important topics. These written communications are typically reviewed by others, including senior colleagues at your firm or company, clients, regulators and other third parties.

Shortly after the 2008–2009 financial crisis, I noticed that the quality of the written communications of our newest hires was slipping and becoming less professional. As I reviewed their work, I continually saw incoherent sentences, poorly organized paragraphs, a lack of substance and even misspellings (despite the existence of spell-check!). Some new staffers also used abbreviations and the slang acronyms that often appeared in text messages. I realized that this generation had grown up with mobile phones and the type of communication protocols that are prevalent in our digital age. However, these professionals need to communicate effectively with Boomers and members of Gen X who are reviewing their work.

I'm a big believer in embracing technology and feel that the advent of text messaging has been a terrific enhancement to the way we communicate with each other. I text all the time with my family members and use many of the common abbreviations and acronyms. However, there is a big difference between these informal, often personal communications and those that professional accountants are responsible for drafting in the business world. Students and young professionals need to understand this distinction and invest the time to develop their writing skills, recognizing that this effort will be an important contributor to their success and advancement.

The Lost Art of "Self-review"

A big step in improving your writing, and an easy one to implement, is to make the time to review your written communications before they are final and given to someone else for review. While this may sound basic, my experience is that it often doesn't take place. Take a few minutes to carefully read through your documents before passing them along. You will find that certain mistakes and problems are apparent and can be corrected by you before someone else sees your documents (and, yes, *use spell-check!*).

The Importance of Speaking Skills

Misunderstandings are quite common in the business world. Sometimes they occur because there was no communication when there should have been. Other times it is because the person being communicated to heard something different than the message or instructions intended by the communicator. This could be because the communicator didn't clearly state the message in a manner that facilitated it being understood, or because the person being communicated to didn't listen very well, or because of both factors. A good way to avoid such misunderstandings is for the communicator to ask a couple of questions after delivering their message or instructions to confirm that the person they are speaking with understands the message. My experience is that it is hard to "over-communicate" but that "under-communication" occurs too often. This is particularly true in a busy, fast-paced world where people are dealing with many competing priorities and easily get distracted.

The Importance of Formal Presentation Skills

As your career advances, you will increasingly find yourself being asked to make formal presentations. For example, you may be asked to address a technical topic with a group of your colleagues. Or perhaps you'll be covering the results of your work at an important meeting with senior management. Maybe you will be asked to give a speech at a conference. One thing is for sure: There will be plenty of times you will be asked to make formal presentations. I lost count years ago of how many presentations I have given in my career, but I conservatively estimate it is over 500.

Given that you can expect to present frequently in your career, why not make it a core competency? Here are a few tips and suggestions that might be helpful in that regard:

- ✓ Take the time to prepare thoroughly.
- ✓ Avoid using too many slides, which can lead to "Death by PowerPoint."
- ✓ Practice.
- ✓ Anticipate and be prepared for likely questions.
- ✓ Know your audience!

The first few times you are asked to make a formal presentation, you may be a bit nervous. This is normal, so don't let it bother you. A good remedy for anxiety is being very well prepared, so convert worry time into prep time! The good news is that you will grow increasingly comfortable as you gain more experience as a presenter.

Interviewing Skills

Many young accountants, particularly auditors, will encounter frequent situations where they are tasked with meeting with clients or others and asking a series of questions to obtain or verify certain information. This can be daunting, particularly if you are somewhat inexperienced. What if the person you are interviewing is much older and more experienced?

What if they are evasive and giving short responses to your questions that aren't very helpful? Good preparation can help you overcome your apprehension. Make the time to think through your objectives for the interview and the specific questions you will ask (Tip: Use a lot of "open ended" questions that don't lend themselves to simple one-word "yes or no" responses). Also, through experience, you will learn the art of following up when the interviewee's response is not satisfactory. You will also develop the important skill of probing, or asking additional questions based on what you learn in response to your earlier questions. Finally, you will learn to ask questions in different ways to corroborate important information.

Becoming a good interviewer is a great way to develop your overall communications skills!

Are You a Good Listener?

Everything covered so far in this chapter is about you being the one who initiates the communication and delivers the message. But it's critically important to realize that good communication is a two-way street. A major part of good communication is being a good listener. In my experience, many people are not. Work on becoming an excellent listener and I'm confident that it will greatly enhance your overall communication skills. Listening may seem like a passive activity, but it does take work and concentration. Most people are so focused on, and thinking about, what they are going to say next in a conversation that they may not be paying attention to what others are saying to them. But if you try to really listen to your colleagues and clients, you will learn a lot, make better decisions, avoid misunderstandings, identify and resolve issues sooner and enhance your working relationships.

To help become a better listener, I encourage you to get into the habit of asking a simple question of those with whom you are interacting: "What do you think?" The benefits of asking this question regularly are significant. First, people appreciate being asked their opinion. Second, they often have something valuable to contribute. But many people, especially if they are reporting to you, may not feel comfortable volunteering their thoughts. So, a little encouragement can go a long way in building a collaborative relationship and getting the benefits of their thinking!

A Communications Lesson I Learned the Hard Way

No one likes to be surprised, particularly when the news is not good. This is especially true in accounting. Early in my career, an audit client of mine had a significant asset that had become impaired, so its book value had to be written down. I communicated this information to the company's chief financial officer and controller and assumed the message had been received and accepted. However, they did not fully agree with my position and didn't even tell the company's audit committee about our view of the matter. When we met with the company's audit committee and mentioned the suggested asset write-down, they were surprised and very unhappy to be learning about it for the first time.

Lesson Learned: Sometimes you need to communicate multiple times, with different constituencies, to ensure that a message has been properly delivered and received.

Food for Thought

The single biggest problem in communication is the illusion that it has taken place.

— George Bernard Shaw, Irish playwright

CHAPTER ELEVEN

Blocking and Tackling: The Importance of Being Organized and Nailing Both Big and Small Tasks

Key Takeaway

Organizational skills should be prioritized as they will be instrumental to your success. Also, make the time to do both the big AND the small things well and on time!

How organized are you? Accountants are responsible for many tasks and responsibilities, both large and small. They typically have specified due dates or "deadlines." Effective professionals develop strategies and techniques for monitoring the status of their work and making sure both the big and little things get done well AND on time. In a technology-enabled world, there are many ways to "keep track of things," including electronic reminders. Maybe you prefer a handwritten "to do" list? The key is to use a system that works for you. This requires both organization and discipline. Sometimes it's easier to focus on the more glamorous aspects of your job but your success will depend on your ability to prioritize appropriately, attend to the full array of your responsibilities and meet important deadlines. As your career advances, well developed skills in these areas will be instrumental to your success.

All jobs encompass a variety of tasks. Some duties, on the surface, may appear unimportant, even mundane. But as a professional you have a responsibility to be diligent in executing tasks that are important to the overall success of your organization.

During my years in public accounting, some of the routine things I was asked to do included:

✓ Completing periodic time and expense reports

✓ Attending continuing professional education (CPE) sessions

✓ Maintaining compliance with the profession's and my firm's independence rules

✓ Completing performance reviews on a timely basis

✓ Billing and collecting cash from our clients

While none of these tasks was glamorous by any means, I learned early in my career that they were vital to the smooth running of our business and that failing to execute them on a timely and consistent basis could create problems. As a result, not paying attention to these "administrative tasks" could get you in trouble. People who consistently appeared on late or non-compliant lists developed a bad reputation. I believe this stemmed from a view that, if you couldn't be trusted to complete small tasks in a timely and efficient manner, how can you be trusted with more important responsibilities?

Similar circumstances exist if you are working for a public or privately owned company or a nonprofit organization. As a lifelong baseball fan, I'll make this analogy: A timely home run can win the big game, but not without your team recording 27 outs on defense, the majority of which will likely come from making the routine plays such as fielding ground balls and catching fly balls. Consistent execution of routine tasks is vital to the success of any business and everyone, including senior executives, has a role to play in this regard. Failure to embrace this important responsibility can sidetrack a career (I have seen it happen multiple times!).

Sometimes the perceived pressures to be constantly focused on client work or other deadlines might seem like a good excuse for some professionals to neglect administrative or other tasks such as obtaining your CPE on a timely basis. Try not to rationalize, as doing so will likely cause problems for you later. Balance and prioritization are important to keep in mind as you navigate your daily to-do list. It is also advisable to always be looking out 2–4 weeks on your calendar to be aware of upcoming due dates.

A good book on this topic is "Coach Wooden's Greatest Secret" (subtitle: "The Power of Little Things Done Well") written by Pat Williams. I am a big college basketball fan and John Wooden was one of my favorite coaches. If you are not familiar with Wooden, many believe he was one of the greatest coaches of all time, having won 10 national championships during his tenure leading UCLA's men's basketball team. Pat's book illustrates the importance of Coach Wooden's philosophy of "sweating the details." John Wooden held himself to high standards and did things in the right way.

Don't Be Late!

Over the course of your professional accounting career, you will be asked to participate in many meetings, conference calls, virtual gatherings and other group activities. Each one will have a designated starting time. Make it a priority to be there on time. In fact, even better, get in the habit of showing up 5–10 minutes early. This is an easy thing to do with a little planning and organization, but I have always been fascinated at how many people are routinely late for scheduled events. While everyone occasionally has an unexpected development disrupt their routine (e.g., an accident on your commute to work causes a traffic jam), don't be "habitually late." It shows a lack of respect for your colleagues. If you do need to be late for a good reason, try to let others know by sending a quick email or text message.

Conversely, routinely showing up "early" shows you are engaged, motivated and that you care about the success of your organization and team. Make it a priority and it will make a difference in your success trajectory.

Effective Meetings

If you are hosting a meeting, make sure people understand the objectives of the meeting and help them be prepared by circulating an agenda in advance. Few things are worse than being asked to attend a meeting where the organizer hasn't really let the attendees know the purpose of the meeting. When the topics of the meeting finally are introduced, people have to react on the spot without having had a chance to think about things in advance or prepare for the discussion. This usually results in a less-than-effective exchange of ideas. Conversely, when people come to a meeting aware of what will be discussed and having had a chance to think about the topics in advance, the discussion is likely to be more fruitful. Plus, sending an agenda in advance shows respect for others' time.

Patience Really Is a Virtue

The accounting profession offers great opportunities and a chance to advance quickly. As soon as you demonstrate you are ready, willing, and able, you will be given more responsibilities. I experienced this continuously throughout my career. But you also must be willing to pay your dues. One of the common perceptions about younger professionals today is that they are eager to advance and always thinking about their next promotion. Neither of these traits is necessarily a bad thing but ambition must be balanced with patience and a recognition that one must master the tasks and role you're in before being ready to advance.

Grow Where You Are Planted

Every organization has assignments that are highly coveted. In a public accounting firm, most professionals want to work on the "premier" clients, whether they be the largest public companies, or the latest, greatest hot technology start-up. These engagements are viewed as offering the best learning experiences, great visibility to showcase your abilities and a chance to be on the "leading edge" of American business. There is nothing wrong with taking advantage of the opportunities provided by these types of assignments, but it is important not to be disillusioned if you're not working on a high-profile assignment. During my career, I had the opportunity to work on a wide variety of client engagements. Some were well-known companies, the kind covered on page one of the *Wall Street Journal*; others were not so high-profile. Over time, I learned that you could expand your knowledge base and strengthen your skills on virtually any client assignment. Rather than complaining about your assigned work, focus on making the most of whatever experience you're being offered.

How My Disappointment Turned into a Learning Opportunity

As a manager, I was assigned to the audit of a local government entity. I was disappointed at first—the engagement was not considered a high-profile client by my colleagues. After a few days of reflection, I decided I was going to make the best of it, work as hard as I could to do a good job for that client and the firm and learn as much as I could about how a local government operates.

It wound up being a terrific experience and, more than three decades later, some of the things I learned on that engagement about how local governments operate are still helpful to me from a civic perspective. An important takeaway from this experience was to focus on the things you can control and not be concerned about the things you cannot control!

Lesson Learned: Make the most of every opportunity.

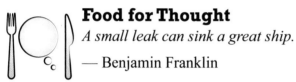

Food for Thought

A small leak can sink a great ship.

— Benjamin Franklin

CHAPTER TWELVE

Have a Value-Creation Mindset

Key Takeaway

Every day, every interaction, presents an opportunity to add (or subtract) value. Be mindful of this reality because, over the long term, your ability to add value will be *the* key determinant of your success. And the more value you add or create, the more successful you will be!

We all regularly shop for a variety of items, including food, clothing and other necessities. Some do it at traditional retail stores; many prefer to do it online. However you choose to shop, you eventually find the item you would like to acquire and then evaluate how much you are being asked to pay for it. Your decision on whether to go ahead with the purchase is based on your judgment about whether the value you're receiving exceeds (or at least equals) the amount you are being asked to pay. Many transactions ultimately don't get consummated because, even though the prospective purchaser would like to acquire an item, they judge it to be overpriced. Stated another way, they are unwilling to give more than they believe they are getting in return. They have not been convinced that the value they are obtaining exceeds the value (purchase price) they are surrendering.

While we can all relate to this concept of evaluating what we are getting in a retail transaction, many people don't appreciate that the same thing takes place in the business world on an everyday basis as employers weigh the value they are deriving from their employees. Think about it!

When you get hired by a firm or company, it is making an initial judgment about your worth to it. While many factors enter into that assessment (including your education and experience and the supply–demand equation in the current marketplace), the employer is essentially wanting to make sure the compensation and fringe benefit costs it will incur in putting you on the payroll is at least equal to (and hopefully less than) the value you will create for the organization. The employer would not hire you if they did not believe the potential existed for you to create value for the business exceeding the cost of employing you. The employer has a continuing opportunity during periodic performance reviews to reassess whether you are creating value. Depending on the employer's judgment about this, it may decide to give you a raise, cut your pay, temporarily furlough you, or terminate your employment.

It is critically important to understand this fundamental economic reality. It's not unique to the accounting profession, but it certainly applies to us. If you want to be successful, get up every day thinking about how you will create value for your employer. I have a great deal of confidence that most employees who create value for their employer on a sustained basis will be rewarded with additional compensation, promotions, increased responsibility, and other opportunities.

Unfortunately, in my experience a lot of people, perhaps the majority, don't possess a "value-creation" mindset. Too often, in fact, they have it backwards. They want or expect their employer to do things for them first, as in, "Give me a good raise and I'll show you what I can do for you." Or "After I get promoted, I'll demonstrate how I can perform at a high level."

A great way to develop a value-creation mindset is to think like an owner. What do I mean by this? Challenge yourself to evaluate how you would handle a situation, or what you might do differently, if it were your business and you personally were going to be directly affected by the outcome. Chances are, you would be laser-focused on being as productive as possible every day if you were self-employed. It should be no different when you are working for someone else. By the way, this is also an excellent guideline to follow when making decisions about business expenses that will be reimbursed by your employer (as in, "Would I be choosing this hotel if it were my own money I was spending?").

There are many ways to create value for your employer; here are a few:

✓ Serve your external (or internal) customer in an exceptional fashion

✓ Identify opportunities for top-line revenue growth for your employer

✓ Assess how a rapidly evolving technology landscape will affect the business

✓ Mentor, motivate and inspire your fellow employees

✓ Figure out ways for the business to operate more efficiently

Regarding the last point, don't hesitate to raise your hand and offer your employer an idea or suggestion on how to improve operations. It's a great way to add value (and to distinguish yourself). Too often, new or relatively inexperienced employees are hesitant to do this. They may see things that they believe can be done better or different, but they are reluctant to communicate their ideas. This could be because they lack confidence or, perhaps, they are not thinking like an owner. They may not appreciate that a "fresh set of eyes" will often spot opportunities to enhance practices that are due for an overhaul. They may also not fully appreciate that there are certain things they may know more about (e.g., social media) than others who have more tenure with the organization. I used to be thrilled when one of our younger professionals at KPMG would ask to see me to share an idea or suggestion. Often, it was a good one we would seek to implement. But even when it wasn't, I would thank the individual and encourage them to keep the suggestions coming!

Myth—Audit Services Are "Commodities"

Certain people believe that audits should be procured for the most inexpensive price possible because the "deliverable"—an opinion on the financial statements of the organization being audited—tends to look fairly similar regardless of the firm doing the work and will generally be acceptable to regulators or other users of the financial statements. They don't understand or appreciate that a high-quality audit can provide value well beyond the opinion in the form of insights on a company's business and a perspective on industry issues or developments that may surface opportunities for the organization. The same often inaccurate view can apply to other types of accounting services, financial systems and certain types of "expert" advice. The old adage "you get what you pay for" certainly applies to professional services. If you focus on getting the lowest price, you are likely to derive the least value!

Look for Opportunities to Provide Feedback

Two of the biggest assets we possess are our technical skills and a "fresh set of eyes." The combination can be extremely powerful if you are willing to take the time to offer feedback. Look beyond the numbers and the basics of tasks you're performing and see the bigger picture. Again, think like an owner. A couple of examples:

✓ You are a junior auditor assigned to review a company's accounts payable process. One of your specific tasks is to develop a flowchart and document procedures used by the client. You will also confirm your understanding of existing workflows by interviewing their personnel. As you walk through their process, ask yourself, "Is there anything that can be done better or differently? What controls can be streamlined or enhanced? Can the process be made more efficient? Is the organization using the data and information generated by the process in a strategic fashion? There are many opportunities to add value if you adopt this mindset.

✓ You are assigned to prepare the individual federal and state tax returns of a high-net-worth individual. As you work through the return, you notice several planning opportunities that, if properly implemented, will enable the taxpayer to save money in the coming year. Do you make the time to schedule a meeting with the client to explain the opportunities? That's added value!

Continually Seek Feedback

Most organizations have a formal annual evaluation process to provide feedback to employees on their performance. Some more progressive organizations do it twice a year. My view is this is way too infrequent to be of value. In a fast-moving business world, you need to be at your best every day. And to perform at a high level, you need frequent feedback. High-performing organizations are getting better at building more frequent feedback loops into the formal HR processes, but most are not there yet. There is a simple solution to this and that is to regularly ask for feedback! Ask your direct supervisor. Ask your client. Ask your colleagues. Most will be willing to be candid and can help you "course correct" sooner rather than later.

Don't Be Afraid to Challenge the Status Quo

Too many people accept the way things are done without thinking critically about whether they can be done better or more efficiently. Get in the habit of adopting a mindset that challenges and questions the status quo. This doesn't mean you seek to be hypercritical. But it does mean that you approach a task with an open mind and are aware of the possibility and potential for improvement. And, if you do identify an issue or problem that needs to be corrected, make an effort to figure out how to address the matter and fix the situation. Leaders help solve problems as opposed to complaining about them! Be a leader and you will be proactively managing your career in a fashion that will help you achieve success.

Environmental Social and Governance (ESG) Considerations

A great way to create value is to stay up to date on the most important issues and challenges your clients or other constituencies you serve are facing. A topic that would be at the top of the list in the current environment is ESG. Investors are appropriately concerned about organizational sustainability and are asking hard questions about topics like carbon emissions, board diversity and proxy voting. Accountants and engaged business advisors should understand this represents an area of opportunity. As more ESG data is compiled and reported to meet investor demands, there will be a need for robust processes, controls and attestation services related to ESG information. This represents a great opportunity for accountants, whether in public or private practice, to add value!

A Case Study in Adding Value

I once met with a company that was seeking to change auditors. The organization was interviewing multiple firms as part of the process. During our meeting, I asked various questions of its management team to develop an understanding of the company's strategic priorities and challenges. In response to one of my questions about its future direction, the company's CFO responded that it was a bit up in the air because the company's two majority owners were seeking to divest their interest in the business. Having gained an understanding of what was effectively the company's biggest issue, I was able to introduce its management team to an individual who put together an investment group to buy out the majority shareholders. This clearly distinguished us from our competition. My firm was hired in large part because we delivered immediate value to this company by helping address its most significant challenge. The new majority owners were also pleased to be introduced to an opportunity that was attractive to them, and the company remained a client of my firm for many years.

Lesson Learned: Always look for opportunities to add value.

Food for Thought

While a fundamental responsibility of business leaders is to create value for shareholders, I think businesses also exist to deliver value to society.

— Kenneth Frazier, CEO, Merck Corporation

CHAPTER THIRTEEN

Embrace Change— Technology Is Your Friend!

Key Takeaway

Change is constant and inevitable, and the pace of change is accelerating. But change is not to be feared; rather it should be welcomed! This is particularly true relative to new and powerful technologies, which have the potential to enhance your performance, productivity and value in the marketplace.

As your career evolves, your success will depend in part on your ability to keep up with the pace of innovation happening in the profession.

You can't avoid hearing about artificial intelligence, robotic process automation, blockchain or other emerging technologies these days. Many pundits believe these technologies will revolutionize accounting and some believe that continuing technology advances will eliminate many jobs in the profession.[27] I believe the first thought is credible but I'm skeptical about the second.

When I started my career in the late 1970s, personal computers (PCs) had not yet been widely deployed and much of the work done by accountants was manual in nature. Although mainframe computers were prevalent in larger companies, some of my smaller clients still actually used manual accounting systems complete with ledgers and journals that made it clear to me where the term "bookkeeper" came from! As auditors, we literally still used pencils and paper and terms such as a "14-column worksheet" were the norm. This landscape changed dramatically in the early to mid-1980s as PCs were rolled out. But it took almost another decade before I had a computer on my desk and began regularly using email as a

---

[27] Roose, K. (2021). "The Robots Are Coming for Phil in Accounting." *New York Times* (6 March), p. B1.

primary means of communicating. Of course, as I write this today, many communications take place via text messaging and social media, and mobile devices have become the preferred medium for communications for many.

Around the same time that the PC came into vogue, electronic spread-sheets (there were several, but I'll use Excel as the one likely to be recognized by most readers) were widely deployed, saving accountants everywhere hours and hours of manual number-crunching. This was a significant technological advance, and it would have been reasonable to assume that Excel would eliminate many accounting jobs. But the opposite has occurred. The number of professional accountants working in the United States and around the world has increased dramatically since the advent of the PC and the Excel spreadsheet. Why? Because these powerful tools have enabled accountants everywhere to use the time the software saved to add more value for their employers and clients in other and different ways. I believe we will see this phenomenon repeat itself in the years to come as some of the new technologies referred to above become mainstream.

Whether you agree with me on this or not, one thing is for sure. Change is constant and will continue. Perhaps you have heard about the well-known Austrian-born Harvard economist, Joseph Schumpeter, who coined the term "creative destruction." He defined it as "the process of industrial mutation that incessantly revolutionizes the economic structure from within, incessantly destroying the old one, incessantly creating a new one." Schumpeter's writings date to the 1940s, an era when manufacturing dominated the economies of the United States and many other nations. Were he expressing the same sentiments today, I am sure Schumpeter would have broadened his "industrial mutation" language to incorporate the notion of rapid technological change in all sorts of enterprises. There are many well-known examples of business models that have become obsolete because of failing to change (Blockbuster video stores and Kodak film come to mind). As I write this, the retail industry continues to be disrupted by Amazon. When I was growing up, Sears was one of the most prominent and respected retailers in the country and the world; it has since filed for bankruptcy. This "creative destruction" will continue and accelerate in an economy where value is increasingly created via intangible versus tangible assets (i.e., think software, patents, and brands!)

Many people fear change but a powerful lesson I learned during my career is that change often brings opportunities for those willing to embrace it. I experienced a great deal of change during my active years in accounting, but I believe those joining the profession today will experience multiples of the change I did (again, because the pace of change is accelerating). Knowing that you probably will be buffeted by change, doesn't it make sense to develop a core competency of effectively dealing with change? Most would say yes but many would also ask, "How?"

Start with these basic principles and strategies:

✓ Don't be surprised by change when it happens (you should always be anticipating it).

✓ Get on the "front end" of a change cycle! Because many fear change they procrastinate dealing with it and wind up behind the change curve, which gives rise to a self-fulfilling prophecy. Better to be an "early adopter" and get out ahead of change.

✓ Volunteer to be a guinea pig. If your organization is testing a new process or technology application and looking for people to try it out, raise your hand.

✓ Make it a priority to continually learn new skills.

✓ Embrace the latest technological advances.

Some Thoughts About Technology

I believe young people entering the workforce today or in the early stages of their careers have a huge advantage when it comes to staying current with technological changes. I say this because they have pretty much grown up with technology and are typically very comfortable with it. Whether it's video games, the latest smartphone feature or a new app designed to enhance productivity, they are used to experimenting, learning, adopting, and taking advantage of new features and applications. Some individuals are even teaching themselves data analytics, coding and programming to build the tools they want if those solutions don't yet exist.

Intellectual Curiosity

Change is less intimidating for those who are intellectually curious. If you are constantly striving to expand your knowledge and skill set, change will come naturally to you. Much of your continuous learning can come from your day-to-day job experiences but it should be supplemented by attendance at formal education sessions that will expose you to new ideas and by a rigorous personal reading program.

Don't Get Too Comfortable

We're all creatures of habit and it's only natural to gravitate to a routine of activities where we feel most comfortable and confident in our abilities. This is especially true after we have "paid some dues" and achieved a level of experience and competence where we feel our hard work and efforts should be rewarded. But to keep pace in a rapidly evolving business world, we need to constantly be stretching out of our comfort zones. Meet new people, expose yourself to new ideas and challenge yourself to learn new things on a regular basis, and you'll have made "adaptability" a core competency! When it comes to technology, continue to experiment and seek to innovate by building on your cumulative knowledge and experience.

A Few Thoughts About Leading in Times of Change

As your career advances, it's likely you will be in a position where you are leading a team or organization through major changes. Here are a few tips that might be helpful in such situations:

✓ Lay out the vision! Explain why the change is necessary and the benefits it will bring.

✓ Repeat the message. People need to hear things more than once for it to sink in.

✓ Be open to their feedback.

✓ Provide frequent updates.

✓ Celebrate progress and achievement of milestones.

It is hard to "over-communicate" with your team in a time of major change, especially because people understandably are concerned about how it will affect them personally. Many leaders make the mistake of under-communicating, which can fuel uncertainty. Get in the habit of reinforcing progress!

A Time When My Role Changed in a Major Way

When I was asked to lead my firm's audit practice, it fundamentally changed my role and daily activities. Although I continued to serve clients, this role was reduced to less than 50% of my time, whereas it had previously occupied virtually all my time. I needed to learn new skills and take on new challenges. I was managing resources and a practice where I now had responsibility for the firm's top-line growth and bottom-line profitability. I was also asked to solve problems and found myself spending much more time interacting with our partners, staff and clients. By being open to these significant changes in my routine, I was able to learn new skills and grow on both professional and personal levels.

Lesson Learned: Change can provide substantial opportunity if you are willing to embrace it!

Food for Thought

When the winds of change blow, some people build walls and others build windmills.

—Chinese Proverb

CHAPTER FOURTEEN

Relationships, Relationships, Relationships

Key Takeaway

Never underestimate the power of personal relationships in helping you achieve a successful accounting career. Make it a priority to devote enough time to develop and nurture them on a regular basis and you'll realize a significant return on the time you invest.

Real estate agents are known to say that "location, location, and location" are the three most important elements in a successful transaction, suggesting that a premier address will drive more demand and a higher price and will probably increase in value over the long term. A similar case can be made that "relationships, relationships, and more relationships" are instrumental to a successful career in the accounting profession. This chapter will address that premise.

Your career will provide you with opportunities to meet many different people. Let's take a look at where and how that might happen:

Coworkers at Your Firm or Company

With all the talk about external networking, sometimes people don't focus on the tremendous opportunity that exists to build relationships within your own organization. This is often where you will find your first mentor or coach, perhaps someone you are working with or for on a regular basis. But it can also be beneficial to get to know coworkers at the same level as you. They are probably dealing with many of the same challenges and opportunities you face and may be a source of good counsel and advice. And make it a point to get to know more senior people at your employer. They may be willing to share their experience with you in a way that can be helpful. Finally, as you gain some seniority, make it a point to connect with those who were hired after you, because these relationships can also be mutually beneficial. During my career, I tried to meet everyone from the newest interns to the most senior partners at the firm, as well as our office support and our administrative team. All of those relationships were often valuable in different ways.

Clients or Customers

Some of the best relationships I developed during my career were with my clients. While always being mindful of my responsibility under professional standards to maintain my objectivity and independence, in both fact and in appearance, I found it was still possible to forge strong bonds with the clients I served. Because I spent a lot of hours with them it's not surprising that, in many cases, we developed mutual respect. These relationships paid dividends throughout my career in terms of referrals and other helpful introductions. After all, who better to vouch for your good work and the value you can add than someone who has first-hand experience working with you?

Vendors and Suppliers

As you gain some seniority with your employer, it's likely you will begin to interact with people from third-party organizations that provide goods or services to your organization or companies you may be jointly serving. I found I was able to build many useful relationships with this group over my career. I can recall one specific situation where I asked the relationship manager from a company that was a vendor to us for an introduction to that organization's chief financial officer. The company eventually became an audit and tax client of my firm.

Alumni from Your Educational Institutions

Many people try to keep in touch with college classmates, and most universities have formal alumni organizations and events. I encourage you to join and participate in your school's alumni organization. This avenue can be particularly valuable early in your career as it will help connect you with more senior and experienced professionals with whom you share a common bond. And don't forget your high school or MBA alumni associations, which can offer similar benefits and contacts. Also, many accounting firms have formal and informal alumni networks that provide a great opportunity to maintain old relationships and establish some new ones.

Professional Associations and Industry Groups

As a CPA, some of the best relationships I built over the years resulted from my involvement with professional organizations, specifically the AICPA and the Pennsylvania Institute of Certified Public Accountants (PICPA). If you are an aspiring CPA, you can become an affiliate member of accounting institutes as a college student, and I encourage you to do so. There are many ways to get involved early in your career with professional groups and other activities that will offer you growth experiences while also expanding your network. You will also be given an opportunity to take on leadership roles that can accelerate your professional development.

If you're not on a CPA track, there will be other professional organizations that will be a good fit for you, depending on your focus. For example, if you're working in the healthcare industry, you might consider joining the Healthcare Financial Management Association. There are similar organizations for professionals in other industries or those specializing in tax or advisory services.

Nonprofit Organizations You Support

Maybe there is a cause that is important to you and your family where you have already been active as a volunteer or donor before launching your professional career (for example, the American Cancer Society, Girl Scouts, United Way, etc.). If so, look to stay involved with these organizations in some capacity, whether it's as a volunteer or board member. If you're not already involved with a nonprofit, you'll find that there are many worthwhile organizations covering a wide range of interests in your area. Find one whose mission appeals to you and that you're willing to invest time supporting. It may be related to the arts or it may be a social services or youth sports organization. In addition to giving back to your community and being involved with a cause you are passionate about, these organizations will help you build relationships and take advantage of leadership opportunities, particularly if you stay involved over time.

Organizations You Belong To

There are many examples, but these might include your church or synagogue, or your local youth sports organization. Again, pick one that aligns with your interests. There are typically a wide range of people involved with these community organizations, but their membership will often include individuals from professions or companies that you might like to meet.

The Importance of Networking

Always look for opportunities to expand your network. There are many events attended by other professionals that will enable you to do this, but it doesn't happen unless you make it a priority. Also, be alert to your surroundings and opportunities they may present. I have met some great people while traveling, simply by striking up a conversation with someone who's seated next to me on an airplane or train.

When you attend an event, don't make the mistake of spending most of your time talking with people you already know. Of course, you don't want to be rude to friends and colleagues and it's fine to say a quick hello to them. But make it a priority to use these occasions to meet new people! Some people still exchange business cards but if you don't get one from the person you meet, you can connect on LinkedIn. Always make it a point to follow up with new connections within 24 hours. While your initial meeting might be brief, a follow-up can offer an opportunity for a more substantive discussion, perhaps over lunch. Many people don't promptly follow up with a new connection and lose the chance to convert it into an ongoing relationship.

In recent years, LinkedIn and other social media sites have become important networking tools. Make sure you keep your profile up to date and utilize social media to proactively develop and maintain your professional relationships.

The Importance of Maintaining Relationships

Once you've built a good relationship with someone, make it a point to stay in touch. This can be hard to do when you have a busy and demanding schedule. Most people make the mistake of not doing so. As a result, their relationships grow stale and eventually lose much of their value. Make the effort to stay in touch with key contacts. While face-to-face interactions are always preferable, you can keep relationships strong in ways that don't require much time, such as sending someone a note or holiday greetings or giving them a call to touch base. Handwritten notes make a big impact, perhaps because they are relatively rare in this digital age.

Involve Others to Help Establish New Relationships

Let's say you would like to meet someone but are unsure how to go about it. You could "cold call" them and ask for a meeting but, absent a compelling value proposition as to why they would want to make the time to do this, that approach may be a long shot. How about a "warm" introduction through an intermediary? That would be someone who you know well who has a good relationship with the person you would like to meet. Your intermediary contacts their friend and requests they meet with you. This can be an effective way of getting to know someone.

The Importance of Helping Others

Relationships are not one-way streets where others are just helping you advance your career. You need to be looking for ways to help others as well. In fact, if you focus on being a resource to others, you will be surprised at how many people begin to seek you out and develop a relationship with you. And, in my experience, most people are inclined to try to reciprocate when you do something for them. It is human nature!

How Keeping in Touch with a Colleague Helped My Firm

Many people start their careers in public accounting but leave to pursue positions in privately owned or publicly owned companies. If I had worked closely with someone who left our firm, I always tried to maintain that relationship by staying in touch with them after they departed. These were people I liked, and I wanted to stay connected.

In one instance, a former colleague of mine had various jobs after leaving our firm. They were doing quite well and were given increasingly important roles as time passed. Although none of the companies this individual worked for was a client of my firm, we stayed in touch. Approximately 20 years after they had departed, this gentleman was working as the CFO of a good-sized public company. That company had occasion to put its audit work out to bid, and my friend called me and invited us to participate. My firm eventually was engaged as the new auditor. While many factors contributed to this outcome, I believe it would not have happened had that CFO and I not stayed in touch over the years.

Lesson Learned: Good things happen when you take the time to build and maintain strong business and personal relationships!

Food for Thought

You can make more friends in two months by becoming interested in other people than you can in two years by trying to get other people interested in you.

—Dale Carnegie, lecturer and author of
    "How to Win Friends and Influence People"

CHAPTER FIFTEEN

Character Traits that Can Help You Succeed

Key Takeaway

It takes more than being smart and gifted to achieve success. There are other key character traits, often in your own control, that can be a differentiator over the course of your career.

A variety of factors can impact career success, and you can expect to encounter twists and turns in the road. Sometimes, you will need to deal with circumstances beyond your control that can delay or frustrate your progress. Occasionally, things work the other way, and you'll be presented with an opportunity you weren't necessarily expecting. A cynic might attribute these events to luck or fate, but I believe there are factors within your control that can greatly increase the likelihood you will be successful over the long term. I'll focus in this chapter on some important traits that I believe can make a huge difference in your ultimate success. It is critical to understand that your unique outlook and the traits discussed below, as well as your behavioral tendencies, can have a significant impact on your work, interactions with others and overall career progress. It is worth noting that none of the factors below is related to your IQ or what university you attended. They are areas anyone can focus on and prioritize and doing so will help you achieve your objectives.

Attitude. I believe the most important of the factors I will discuss in this chapter is your attitude. By the way, it's critical to realize that your attitude can be either an asset or a liability. I've met many individuals during my career whose "bad" attitudes derailed their career progression. Conversely, a positive attitude can be instrumental to your success. Having a positive attitude doesn't mean you don't occasionally get frustrated, disappointed or upset with difficult circumstances. It is quite human to experience these emotions as we wrestle with the ups and downs of our daily worklife. But professionals who consciously cultivate a positive attitude don't dwell on negative emotions or allow them to dominate their thinking. This doesn't mean being naive. Professionals with good attitudes possess a particular ability to recognize both challenges and opportunities and to deal with difficulties in a constructive fashion. Even when faced with a daunting situation, their thinking revolves around answering the question: "How can I improve this situation?" as opposed to: "It's so unfair that I have been put in this situation!"

Professionals who have a positive attitude also get in the habit of periodically reflecting on the things that are going well. That is a list that is much longer than many of us at first realize but, human nature being what it is, we tend to take some of those things for granted.

The best observation I can offer with respect to attitude is that you aren't necessarily born with a "good" or "bad" attitude. Rather, your attitude is shaped by your daily thoughts, and you can consciously manage those thoughts. Do so to your advantage!

Empathy. As discussed in Chapter Nine, you'll spend a high percentage of your time in the field of accounting working with others. Your ability to do so in a collaborative fashion is essential to your success. This becomes even more important as your career advances and you begin to lead projects and teams. While there are many traits that are important to working effectively with others (e.g., cooperation, honesty, respect, etc.), I would put empathy near the top of the list. Empathy is defined as "the ability to understand and share the feelings of others."[28] I think a good way to think about empathy is "putting yourself in someone else's shoes." What is the other person dealing with currently, not just in their job, but in their personal life? If you are totally insensitive or unaware of their situation, chances are you will have a difficult time relating to them and, ultimately, building a relationship. On the other hand, something as simple as periodically asking a colleague, "How is it going?" and taking a few minutes to listen to their response, can be a huge factor in developing positive relationships, trust, and loyalty. This small amount of effort is an investment well worth making. Never underestimate the power and satisfaction that comes from making this kind of connection with others. In a busy, fast-moving professional business environment, many people don't take the time to connect. But if you do so, it will make a positive difference in your career advancement.

Myth—Nice People Finish Last

The saying "nice guys finish last" is often attributed to Leo Durocher, who managed several major league baseball teams. In fact, he wrote a book with that title. During my career, I met many nice people (men and women) who were very successful. So, don't buy into the notion that you can't be nice and successful and remember the adage: "It's nice to be important but it's more important to be nice!"

Commitment. While it might take you a number of years after launching your professional career to decide what your long-term goals look like, the ability to commit to them once they're established can, in my experience, be an important factor in your long-term success. Another way to think about this is, "How bought-in are you?" Dedication to a long-term goal is a common trait of successful people in virtually all occupations and

---

[28] *Merriam-Webster Dictionary.*

professions, from athletes to artists. Accountants who are committed to advancing in the profession go the extra mile. They volunteer to take on additional responsibility. They demonstrate "intellectual curiosity" about subjects that are relevant to their firms or companies and career. They pay attention to developments affecting their profession and develop a point of view on those issues. In short, they are both engaged and proactive in their approach to their careers. They give speeches, write articles, and teach courses. As their careers advance, they sit on nonprofit boards. In summary, they are thought leaders who are willing to "jump into the fray" and make a difference, and this positions them well to continue to advance and achieve their long-term goals.

Hard Work. I have never met a successful accounting professional who did not possess a strong work ethic. There are no shortcuts, and you must be willing to roll up your sleeves and invest the time and energy to master your craft. So, be prepared to pay your dues! But as discussed in Chapter Five, don't believe all the horror stories about working 80-hour weeks consistently or toiling nights and weekends throughout the year.

Initiative. Are you willing to take action to accelerate the achievement of your goals? Ordinary employees "do what is expected" but don't necessarily go above and beyond the call of duty. The dictionary defines initiative as "energy or aptitude displayed in initiation of action" as in "she showed great initiative!" People with this trait are always seeking new and additional responsibilities. Fortunately, in the accounting profession there are plenty of opportunities for those who put their hands up and ask to take on more responsibility. Those who take advantage of these opportunities will accelerate their learning curve and career growth. They will also distinguish themselves in a fashion that contributes to being considered for special assignments or leadership roles.

Perseverance. Are you willing to keep trying when the chips are down? When others are ready to throw in the towel? Are you relentless in continuing to pursue your goals, even when things are not going well? Many people give up when they encounter obstacles, so the ability to consistently persevere will set you apart over time. Perseverance is defined as "persistence in doing something despite difficulty or delay in achieving success." While the concepts of focus and commitment, addressed above, have some similarities to perseverance, I think the word "persistence" is key to understanding this definition. It means you keep coming back when others give up. A friend of mine, Jim Maguire, who built a remarkably successful company in the insurance industry, wrote a book on the story of his life and career which really drives home this point. Jim entitled his book: "Just Show Up Every Day!" The basic concept was that if you hang in there and persevere, good things will happen!

Resilience and Mental Toughness. How effectively do you deal with adversity? All of us experience it from time to time, in varying degrees. You will certainly encounter setbacks during your career, so developing the ability to bounce back after you've been knocked down is an extremely important asset. Resilience isn't necessarily an innate trait: It takes practice. Sometimes a disappointment, such as not getting promoted after you have worked extremely hard and feel as if you earned it, can be difficult to handle. But having a long-term view and keeping things in perspective will help you remain calm and professional in even the most challenging circumstances. Resilience is defined as "the capacity to recover quickly from difficulties; toughness." Sometimes, the line between perseverance and resilience is a fine one. While these important traits have some similarities, I believe the major distinction is that resilience enables you to effectively deal with short-term disappointments or challenges, whereas perseverance is a long-term state of mind.

Teamwork. How effectively do you interact with your colleagues? More than ever before, the need to collaborate with others in accomplishing a mutual goal is an important attribute for success in the accounting profession. To be a team player, it cannot be "all about you." You need to understand and contribute to the goals of the team, which often starts with doing things that will help your colleagues be successful. That can mean being willing to make personal sacrifices for the benefit of the group. There is an old saying in business that comes to mind: "It's amazing how much can be accomplished when no one is worried about who gets the credit."

Grit. The dictionary defines this term as "firmness of mind or spirit; unyielding courage in the face of hardship or danger."[29] While it is similar to the concepts of resilience and mental toughness discussed above, and also embodies perseverance, there has been some pioneering research done in recent years regarding how important this grit can be to success. Angela Duckworth, a professor of psychology at the University of Pennsylvania, has written a book on the topic if you are interested in learning more in this area.[30]

Emotional Intelligence. EI is the capability of individuals to recognize their own emotions and those of others, discern between different feelings and label them appropriately, use emotional information to guide thinking and behavior and adjust emotions to adapt to environments. While the term is not new, it gained popularity in a 1995 best selling book, "Emotional Intelligence," by Daniel Goleman. He defined EI as the ability to identify, assess, and control one's own emotions, the emotions of others, and that of groups.[31] Again, there are some similarities to the concept of empathy discussed above. The concept of EI also incorporates the idea of being "self-aware," which the dictionary defines as "having conscious knowledge of one's own character, feelings, motives and desires."[32] In a profession that entails frequent interaction with other people, regardless of your choice of terminology, these skills and concepts will be important to your success!

---

[29] *Merriam-Webster Dictionary.*

[30] Duckworth, A. (2016). *Grit: The Power of Passion and Perseverance.* New York: Scribner.

[31] Goleman, D. (1995). *Emotional Intelligence: Why It Can Matter More Than IQ.* New York: Penguin Random House.

[32] *Oxford Dictionaries.*

A Final Tip: Don't Make Excuses. Sometimes, things go wrong despite our best efforts and occur for reasons that are beyond your direct control. When this happens, it is easy to "make excuses," blame others or complain that "it wasn't your fault." Don't fall into that trap! Successful people accept responsibility. When you do so, others will notice and admire you for it (they are often aware of the circumstances that you would have used as your excuse without you bringing them up).

Dealing with a Disappointment in My Career

I recall being informed by one of my firm's senior partners in Philadelphia that I was performing at a high level and had all the qualifications to become a partner with the firm. In fact, the Philadelphia office partners as a group had nominated me for partner. The next step in the process was to obtain the approval of the firm's executive office. This approval would be dependent in part on demonstrating an appropriate "business case" for the promotion.

About six months later, I was informed that our executive office had not approved my promotion because the business case could not be supported (this was during a period when we were experiencing slow growth and no partners were retiring, so that was probably reasonable). I was disappointed because I felt I was ready to be a partner. Unfortunately, that same process repeated itself the following year. But because I was committed to my long-term goal, I persevered and finally made partner in the third year.

Lessons Learned: This experience underscored the tremendous importance and value of embracing a variety of the traits described above, including attitude, commitment, perseverance, resilience, mental toughness and grit! It also is a good reminder of another important concept when navigating your career journey: Think long term and don't be discouraged by short-term setbacks!

Food for Thought

Luck is what happens when preparation meets opportunity.

— Seneca, Stoic philosopher

Section Three

Building on Your Success as Your Career Advances

CHAPTER SIXTEEN

How to Avoid Burnout

Key Takeaway

Over the course of your career, there will be times where you feel uninspired, worn down, overwhelmed and perhaps "tired of your job." There are steps you can proactively take to avoid or minimize these situations and effectively deal with them when they do occur.

"Burnout" is a condition defined as "exhaustion of physical or emotional strength or motivation, usually because of prolonged stress or frustration."[33] While burnout is certainly not a condition unique to the accounting profession (it also frequently occurs in other occupations, such as law or healthcare), many accountants I have worked with during my career told me they were experiencing burnout. A high percentage of them eventually changed jobs and some of them left the profession.

Why do many accountants experience burnout? Well, we know that the profession can require periods of sustained overtime. We also know that accountants are often working under tight deadlines, and that can create stress. Certainly, these factors, among others, can contribute to feeling overwhelmed.

Some accountants let burnout happen to them without engaging in proactive strategies to avoid it. This chapter will offer some tips, ideas, and suggestions on avoiding burnout, or, as I like to say, keeping your batteries charged.

---

[33] *Merriam-Webster Dictionary.*

Variety Is the Spice of (Working) Life

Individuals are more subject to feeling burned out when they are over-worked and feeling the constant pressure of looming deadlines, a situation that can occur frequently in the accounting profession. People also some-times get burned out when they are doing the same work over and over with little variety or challenge. This might happen, for instance, if you are working for a company and oversee the monthly closing of the books. Each month you follow the same process and procedures, work with the same reports and information and deal with pretty much the same people. It is easy to become bored in these circumstances and that boredom can evolve into frustration and, eventually, burnout.

How to avoid falling into this trap? Ask for new, more challenging assignments! Train someone else to do your job. Take on a special project. If these opportunities are not available at the company or firm you work for, consider changing jobs.

Interesting and challenging work will keep you mentally stimulated. As you learn new tasks and tackle new projects, you'll increase your confidence as well as your value to your employer and in the external marketplace.

Satisfaction and Sense of Accomplishment

Maybe related to the previous point, your work should provide you with a sense of satisfaction and accomplishment. We all need to feel comfortable that we're using our time in a productive fashion and that, ideally, our work matters and makes a difference. Doing something new or different effec-tively provides a sense of accomplishment which can keep you motivated. This is one of the reasons that continuous learning is essential to long-term career success. Achievement also provides psychological rewards.

Constant stress and long hours, on a sustained basis, can also diminish your overall level of satisfaction with your job. To be clear, and as discussed in Chapter 5, a certain level of overtime is normal and should be expected. Also, accounting is a profession driven by deadlines and there will always be pressure to achieve them. Effectively planning, managing, and executing an engagement or project to satisfy a deadline can actually be a rewarding experience and provide a sense of accomplishment. But if you are moving from one stressful deadline to the next and constantly feeling "under the gun," the risk of becoming burned out increases. Recognize that you can proactively manage that risk! Following are some techniques to help you do so.

Unplug!

Cellphones, email and text messaging are great when it comes to facilitating communication. But, as with many things in life, their use needs to be moderated and managed. This is more necessary than ever in the "24-by-7, on-demand" world we live in. If you are constantly checking your phone or computer for new messages, even on nights and weekends, it is going to be extremely hard to relax and take your mind off work for a while. You need some downtime to stay fresh. Get in the habit of unplugging even if you need to force yourself to do so in the beginning. Remember, your devices are the tools, not the boss.

Compartmentalize

Related to the preceding section, try focusing fully on your professional duties while doing your job but on your family, hobbies or self when not working. In recent years, this has been extremely hard for many people to do given the increasing power of technology and the world being so connected. It has become perhaps even more challenging during the pandemic when many professionals are working from their homes and separating work and personal life can be difficult as those lines continue to blur. But there are clear mental health benefits to giving yourself a break from work and focusing on other things can help you be more productive and effective when you do reengage on work-related matters.

Don't Let Your Work Consume You

Many of the people I've known who eventually suffered from burnout had fallen into the trap of being totally absorbed by their job, to the exclusion of virtually all other aspects of their life. Perhaps you've heard the proverb "All work and no play make Jack (or Jill) a dull boy (or girl)"

It's very important to make time for your family and friends and doing the things you enjoy. It is also helpful to have a hobby that will take your mind off work and let you mentally recharge. Whether the activity is playing or watching sports, going to the museum or the theatre, playing video games or just hanging out with your friends and family, find some diversion from your day job.

Learn How to Say No

Highly motivated people are more likely to assume responsibility and volunteer for "extra" assignments. This is fine to a point. But as your career progresses, you will find that you develop a reputation for being a "go-to" person. This will result in more requests to take on responsibilities or activities beyond your regular duties. Most people rightly feel honored when asked to do something "extra." It is an indication your employer thinks highly of you and has confidence in your abilities. But, if you agree to do too many things, your personal life will suffer, and you'll increase the possibility of burning out. Successful people need to master the art of saying no!

Stay Physically Fit

The dictionary definition of burnout cited above refers to "exhaustion of physical strength." When you are working long hours and not taking good care of yourself, it's easy to become run down and, if this occurs on a sustained basis, it can lead to burnout.

It is important to develop a physical fitness routine and prioritize it. A proper diet and good sleep habits are essential to both your emotional and physical well-being.

Stay Mentally Fit

Even in your busiest period, it's important not to be one-dimensional. If you never make the time to do anything but read accounting publications or pronouncements or prepare tax returns, you are more likely to burn out. Even if you spend a good part of your day on work-related activities, make the time to go to a movie or sporting event, to watch the evening news or take advantage of other diversions you enjoy. It will keep you sharp.

Stay Emotionally Fit

Make time for your loved ones. First of all, you owe it to them. But also, the time you invest with them will help take your mind off your work. And their support and encouragement will help you navigate challenging and stressful times at work.

Stay Spiritually Fit

This is not intended to be a religious commentary but most of us have a spiritual side and we ignore it at our own peril. Just as staying physically, mentally, and emotionally fit is important, it's critical to make enough time to devote to whatever that spiritual side looks like for you.

How Balls and Bats Gave Me a Break

For a good part of my career, I had the opportunity to coach youth sports. I coached baseball, basketball and soccer (which kept me engaged pretty much year-round) for kids from ages 6 to 17. I really enjoyed doing this and it was a great way for me to take my mind off work. No matter how challenging a day I may have had, or whatever difficult issues I was wrestling with, when I got to the field, those kids needed my total attention. By focusing on them for a few hours, I was able to give my mind a break from pressing work issues. Usually, when I reengaged on my work the next morning, I did it with a fresh mind and perspective, which helped me more effectively deal with whatever challenges I was facing.

The old adage that no one lying on their death bed ever said, "Gee, I wish I had worked a few more hours" is accurate and important to keep in mind!

Lesson Learned: Work hard, but don't overcommit to your career to the detriment of your personal life.

Food for Thought

I'm a big believer of work–life balance. You need a little downtime to recharge to make sure that when you are here, you're really all here. I still have a child in high school, so I go to her sporting events, even if it means leaving work and working again when I get home.

—Mary Barra, CEO of General Motors

CHAPTER SEVENTEEN

Career Transitions: How to Make Good Decisions

Key Takeaway

Virtually every individual working in the accounting profession will need to make critical career decisions concerning whether to stay with their current employer or leave for a new opportunity. Many will need to make these decisions multiple times over the course of a career. There can be good reasons to leave for a new opportunity but be sure you objectively and rigorously evaluate your decision with the long-term in mind before making a final decision.

There are many reasons an employer-employee relationship can come to an end. Unfortunately, the separation is sometimes initiated by the employer, as is the case with a layoff or termination for cause. Much more frequently, however, the change is initiated by the employee, ideally for good reasons. Sometimes, however, employees leave for the wrong reasons. This chapter will focus on important considerations to address when you're contemplating a career transition.

Over my career, I probably met with more than 100 people who were considering leaving my firm to discuss their thought process and rationale. These folks were at all levels of the firm, from relatively new associates (one or two years of experience) to partners. Each situation was unique. Many were well prepared for our conversations; it was clear to me they had thought things through. Others, not so much—their decision seemed to be based more on fleeing what they viewed as a bad (short-term) situation. Some had received unsolicited job offers from a client. Others had responded to a call from a headhunter. And, more than a few initiated a job search because they were feeling "burnt out" after a challenging busy season. Most of the people I met with did leave the firm. In a small number of cases, maybe 10% or so, they decided to stay.

There are some particularly good reasons to leave your current employer; here are a few:

✓ You have stopped learning and growing.

✓ You are in a toxic culture, working with individuals who don't share your values.

✓ Your employer seems unconcerned about your future.

✓ You continue to be assigned to work that you have done previously and mastered.

✓ You are not being compensated fairly.

And there are some extremely poor reasons for leaving, including:

✓ You are reacting to a disappointment.

✓ You will make more money (in the short term).

✓ You will work fewer hours (in the short term).

✓ You will get more vacation or other fringe benefits (in the short term).

Let's take a closer look at eight important things to keep in mind when evaluating major career decisions.

1—Make your employer aware of your concerns

If you're thinking about leaving, there may be specific factors motivating you to do so. Perhaps you have been working long hours for a sustained period or are being asked to travel extensively. Maybe the assignments you have been working on aren't particularly challenging or interesting. You should alert the appropriate people at your employer to these concerns. Often, they can address your issues and may be willing to do so. Too many professionals abruptly resign without having a good discussion with their employer about their situation and what is motivating them to consider leaving. From an employer's perspective, most are focused on retaining talent. Today, employers have evolved to the point where most are more flexible to discuss employee concerns, particularly if you are viewed as a strong performer. I recall a situation where one of my colleagues wanted to pursue an MBA, and we made appropriate modifications to their schedule and workload to make doing so feasible. That person not only stayed with the firm and earned the MBA, but later was promoted into a leadership role with the firm. Talking with your employer about your concerns is almost always a good idea. Even if you still leave, your firm will not feel blind-sided when you resign, which will contribute to you leaving on good terms.

2—Consult with others

You may think your decision is straightforward, perhaps even obvious. Even so, you will generally benefit from talking it through with other people you trust and respect. This could include family members, a spouse or good friend, as well as professional colleagues at various levels. Individuals who aren't as close to a situation as you are can sometimes offer different and valuable perspectives and raise questions you may not have considered. When I was early in my career, I was working a lot of hours and traveling a fair amount. I received a call from a search firm about an opportunity in private industry that sounded attractive. I interviewed and was offered the position. Fortunately, I spoke with a senior manager I worked for about my decision and he raised a lot of great points I had not thought about. This convinced me to turn down the job and stay with the firm. I believe this turned out to be a good decision.

One of the lessons I learned in my career was that it was almost always valuable to consult with others when faced with a difficult decision.

3—Explore other options with your current employer

Let's say you have completed two or three years on the audit staff of your firm and are thinking that being an auditor is not your preferred long-term career path. Before seeking opportunities outside your firm, you may want to explore whether you could transfer to another group within the firm, such as the advisory practice. I have seen many individuals do this over my career. The bigger the firm, the more diverse the opportunities may be. If your firm is large, with global operations, you might also want to look into executive-office assignments or international rotations, which can not only offer a change of pace in the short term but also be steppingstones to other opportunities down the line.

4—Think long term

Maybe the most important question to ask yourself is "What are the longer-term ramifications of this decision?" I have seen far too many people leave for a small increase in compensation in the short term when staying a few more years would have increased their earnings potential significantly over the long term. In one instance, someone with a couple of years of experience accepted a relatively low-level position as an internal auditor with a large company. While the new position resulted in a double-digit pay raise initially, the rate of compensation increases slowed significantly in the ensuing years. Perhaps more significantly, the nature of the work they were asked to perform in this role was less challenging. Similarly, I have seen people take a new position that didn't offer the continuous learning and growth opportunities that staying at their prior employer would have. Leaving "too soon" can hurt the long-term trajectory of your career. A good question to ask yourself is: "How might taking this position affect me five or ten years in the future?"

Myth—I'm Sure I'll Make More Money if I Leave

During my career, I've known many people who have chosen to leave public accounting after a year or two because they could earn more working in industry. While they may get a good raise when they change jobs, they often do not make more money over the long term.

5—Perform "due diligence" on your prospective employer

It's essential to do some research on a company or firm you are considering joining, particularly if it isn't a well-known organization. I once had someone come into my office to resign. The company they joined declared bankruptcy within a week of their start date. The person called me and asked for his old job back. We were able to help, but this individual would have been much better off had he done his homework on the prospective employer before accepting the position. With so much information available online these days, it is easy to do some research on a prospective employer. While you are at it, see what you can also find out about the team you are going to be working with (look at their LinkedIn profiles, etc.). It's also helpful to consider and endeavor to understand the culture of the organization you are considering joining. And see if you can meet with several of your prospective colleagues during the interview process to gain some insight into their personalities and values. Pay attention to cultural cues during these discussions and make an assessment as to what extent they are focused on their people. If possible, validate your understanding by speaking with people who worked for the company in the past or that deal with them currently.

6—Develop a balanced scorecard

When someone is considering resigning, it's often because they're focused on aspects of their current situation that aren't optimum. But it's important not to rush to judgment without considering what is "good" about the present situation. Maybe it's just human nature to put more weight on negative than positive factors, but both should be evaluated in an objective fashion. For instance, if your present employer offers "world-class" training, that could be an especially important consideration in a fast-paced business world where continuous learning and growth will be important to your future success. I believe the time-tested approach recommended by Benjamin Franklin[34] of making up a list of pros and cons of your current situation, then weighing their relative importance, is always a worthwhile exercise. Listing the pros and cons will help you reach a well-informed and thoughtfully considered judgment. It will also assist you in evaluating a potential opportunity through the essential lens of your personal values and priorities. By the way, take the time to also consider whether any of the "con" factors can be addressed and resolved to your satisfaction. Perhaps you can tackle one of the issues yourself with a little creative thinking or maybe talking with your employer about your concerns (as recommended above) will eliminate one or more of the "con" factors. In either event, this extra step could influence the outcome and provide a sense of satisfaction that you were able to successfully resolve an important concern in a manner that improved your career outlook.

7—Personal considerations

Much of the preceding discussion focuses on the implications of staying or leaving for your professional career. But what about your personal life? This is just as important, if not more so, as your career. If your present job is negatively affecting your family or personal relationships, you should strongly consider making a change. In most families today both parents

---

[34] Letter from Franklin to Joseph Priestly, September 19, 1772. Founders Online, National Archive. https://founders.archives.gov/documents/Franklin/01-19-02-0200

work, so childcare is also an important consideration. Families with single parents face similar challenges. The good news is many employers have become more flexible in helping employees juggle their professional and personal lives. But my view is that you should avoid putting your job in front of your family on a long-term basis. There will certainly be periods where work will be a priority in the short term, but those situations should be periodic versus permanent. In certain situations, you may have to remain in a position temporarily to continue to pay your bills. But if your personal life is consistently suffering over a multi-year period, prioritize developing and implementing your exit strategy!

8—Don't burn bridges

Assuming that you do decide to leave an employer, it is important to handle the transition process in a professional and courteous fashion. This includes giving adequate notice (which often can be more than two weeks, depending on your level within the organization and your responsibilities, including the projects you're working on). I once had a partner attempt to resign on extremely short notice even though our firm's partnership agreement required six months' notice and we were in the midst of a very busy time for the firm. In other instances, I saw people provide more notice than was required so they could see an important project through to completion. In most cases, your new employer will support, respect and appreciate you handling the transition in a professional way, even if they have to wait a bit longer for you to start there.

A "Stay or Leave" Decision I Had to Make

I received an unsolicited job offer from a public company client of my firm after I had been in public accounting for about seven years. The position offered to me included an increase of about 25% in my base compensation, a company car and stock options. It was an extremely attractive offer financially and I may have experienced a decrease in the hours I was working had I accepted the position. I thought long and hard about that opportunity. I had two young children at that time and the extra money and free time would have helped a lot. But I ultimately declined the position. As I reflected on my circumstances, I realized that I enjoyed what I was doing and was continuing to learn and grow in my position with the firm. I also felt that, on a longer-term basis, my career and financial prospects were good. Looking back at that decision, I have no regrets and think I made the right call!

Lesson Learned: Think long term!

Food for Thought

What is it you like doing? If you don't like it, get out of it, because you'll be lousy at it. You don't have to stay with a job for the rest of your life, because if you don't like it, you'll never be successful in it.

—Lee Iacocca, former CEO of Chrysler

CHAPTER EIGHTEEN

The Importance of Giving Back

Key Takeaway

No one achieves success without a lot of help from others, and we all have a responsibility to assist those who follow us. As your career advances, make it a priority to help those who come behind you and look for opportunities to contribute to the broader community where you live and work. Besides being the right thing to do, helping others is tremendously rewarding. You have valuable skills to share!

Every one of us has a unique story. But I think it is very rare for someone to be able to legitimately claim that 100% of their accomplishments were due to their own merit and efforts and that they received no help along the way. Conversely, many of us had quite a bit of assistance from our parents or other family members, teachers, mentors, and friends during our formative years. The assistance might have been monetary, as in helping to finance your education, but likely also involved guidance and encouragement as you contemplated your potential field of study and career path. Perhaps once you had decided on a chosen career, someone working in the profession took a personal interest in you and made the time to answer questions you had or provide other advice. They might even have made a call or two to help you secure an internship or serve as a reference. Maybe a supportive spouse made sacrifices that helped you pursue your dreams. Or you received a scholarship with tuition assistance from a nonprofit organization. I suspect one or more of these scenarios applies to most of those reading this.

If you've been the beneficiary of someone else's efforts to help you succeed, make sure you express your gratitude, not just once, but on an ongoing basis. Stay in touch with the people and organizations that helped you and keep them apprised of your career progress. They will appreciate it!

Just as important, you should begin thinking, early on, about how you can "pay it forward" to the younger professionals who follow you. There will be many opportunities to do so in your future.

Early in your career, you will be able to start helping others. It is likely, after a couple of years of experience at your firm or company, that you will find yourself in a supervisory role that provides multiple opportunities to assist individuals who are just starting their careers. If you are functioning as a senior or in-charge accountant on an engagement, "on the job training" is a major part of your responsibilities and a great opportunity to develop your supervisory and listening skills. You will still be performing day-to-day work yourself at this point, but don't make the mistake of viewing answering questions and providing guidance to newer staff as a distraction that slows you down. On the contrary, it is a very important part of your job to serve as a resource for colleagues. You can provide short, curt answers to questions or you can take the time to really explain things to your coworkers and help connect their work to the bigger picture. Sure, the latter approach requires more time and effort but your subordinates, your firm and your client will benefit in the long run (and so will you!). In fact, making the time to provide effective supervision is actually an investment in your future, because overseeing the work of others will become a bigger part of your job responsibilities in the future and will be critical to your success (so you'll want to get very good at doing it!).

As your career progresses, you will find yourself in an excellent situation to provide coaching and other career advice to your younger colleagues. You may also be able to directly impact the quality of their work experience by offering flexibility, to the extent practical, to help with their work–life balance. You can likely also provide critical support for younger team members as they encounter some of the more challenging aspects of an accounting career for the first time.

You can also serve as an instructor at training programs offered by your firm or company. This is a great way to share your knowledge and experience with the next generation.

Another great vehicle to start to give back early in your career is returning to your alma mater to spend time with students. Perhaps you could speak to the accounting society or your university's Beta Alpha Psi chapter about your early-career experiences. Maybe your school has a mentoring or mock interview program. Any of these options would enable you to share your experience and insight with those preparing to enter the profession. Chances are that you benefited from someone doing this for you when you were still a student. Eventually, you will have a chance to give back. It is time well spent.

Opportunities Outside of Work

As your career advances there will be opportunities to get involved with organizations outside the company or firm where you work to volunteer and help others. Pick an entity whose mission you can relate to and will be passionate about. In my experience, nonprofits are always looking for people with accounting skills, and this may position you to gain leadership experience and perhaps even join a board early in your career. Also, as discussed in Chapter 14, your involvement can also be beneficial from the standpoint of building relationships. But those things should not be your principal motivation in getting involved. Rather, your focus should be on giving back and helping others.

What causes interest you? Pick an organization where you can not only give back but be fully engaged in the work because you believe in what it is trying to accomplish. Here is a short list of possible candidates:

✓ Your church or religious organization

✓ A local youth sports organization

✓ The Boy Scouts or Girl Scouts

✓ The United Way

✓ The American Cancer Society, The American Heart Association, or similar organizations

✓ A civic organization

✓ An arts or culture organization

✓ Your local school board

✓ A professional organization, such as your state CPA society

You get the idea. There are many organizations that can benefit from your skills, energy and experience. Pick the one that is right for you and get involved!

My experience was that, as my career progressed, even though my responsibilities and the demands on my time increased in many ways, I had more opportunities to give back. Perhaps this was related to the fact that you tend to have more control over your own schedule as you become more senior within your organization. It probably also is a function of my accumulated experience and contacts.

Serving as an Adjunct Professor

If you have the time to teach an accounting or tax class at a college in your area, you'll have the opportunity to touch young lives in a powerful way and perhaps be a resource to them as they contemplate their professional future. Teaching is also a great way to keep your own skills sharp; you'll benefit from class preparation and almost certainly learn a few new things from your students!

Making Young People Aware of Careers in Accounting

Many high schools and community colleges have "career days" when they invite guest speakers to come to their schools and talk to the students about their profession. This is a great way to give back and potentially encourage a young person to pursue a career in accounting.

Mentoring

Many organizations have formal mentoring programs where you can volunteer to be a mentor. There is nothing wrong with this and I wouldn't discourage you from participating. But, in my experience, many mentoring relationships develop naturally without an organized structure or format. Be open to these opportunities as they arise. Make time to help others. You will benefit in the long run.

Other Ways to Give Back

During my career, I've received dozens of calls from former colleagues or clients who were "in transition." It could be that their companies were downsizing or restructuring, resulting in workforce reductions. Maybe their employer had been acquired or was filing for bankruptcy. Whatever the circumstances, they were trying to find their next position and networking is an important aspect of any job search. I always tried to take these meetings and be helpful to the person looking for a position.

It does not require a lot of time to meet with someone to understand the situation and what they are looking for, then maybe make a few phone calls or an introduction on their behalf. Sometimes, this can result in a real "win-win" situation where a company you know has a need it is trying to fill and the person who is in transition happens to be a good fit for that position. While that does not happen often, something as simple as introducing the job seeker to other good networking contacts can be extremely helpful to their search and is usually greatly appreciated.

A Great Opportunity I've Had to Give Back

Since retiring from KPMG a few years ago, I have had the opportunity to become involved at Rowan University in southern New Jersey serving as an "Executive in Residence." This role enables me to deliver guest lectures to the students on a variety of topics. I have chaired the University's Accounting Advisory Board and spend time mentoring and coaching students as they prepare to transition from the academic world into the professional world. It has been both an enjoyable and rewarding experience.

Lesson Learned: Helping others can be tremendously satisfying and rewarding.

Food for Thought

From those to whom much has been given, much is expected.

—John F. Kennedy, paraphrasing the *Gospel of St. Luke*

Afterword

It has been fun putting my thoughts on paper for this book. As I have said to a few folks who inquired about my motivation for this project, it wasn't to "make money" or produce a bestseller. Rather, my sincere hope is that the book can be helpful in some small way to the targeted audience. If only a handful of individuals derive benefit from the advice herein, my investment of time will have been well worth it!

If you found the book to be helpful, do me a favor and share some of the advice with a friend, fellow student, or colleague.

By way of summarizing the key concepts covered throughout the book—and in hopes of provoking thought and hopefully action by the reader—I have listed below 50 questions that I hope will serve as a good synopsis of the material covered throughout the book.

Chapter 1: Why Accounting Is a Great Profession

✓ Would you like to position yourself for a variety of financially rewarding career opportunities?

✓ Is a career that provides a high degree of flexibility an important priority for you?

✓ Do you like to be involved in making decisions?

Chapter 2: Is Becoming a CPA the Right Path for You?

✓ Have you evaluated the advantages and disadvantages of pursuing 150 credit hours?

✓ Do you understand credentialing alternatives, and have you considered your preferences?

✓ Do you plan to begin your career as an auditor working in public accounting?

Chapter 3: How Accounting Majors Can Optimize the College Experience

✓ Are you taking advantage of all the resources and initiatives your school offers?

✓ What is your strategy to secure an internship during your college years?

Chapter 4: Career Paths

✓ Is there an industry that you are passionate about and would like to target?

✓ Where do you see yourself ten years from now from an "ideal job" standpoint?

✓ How will you ensure you stay challenged and continue to grow throughout your professional career?

Chapter 5: What About Work–Life Balance?

✓ Are you giving thought to the full spectrum of your personal and professional goals?

✓ Have you evaluated what type of professional role might be best for you?

Chapter 6: The Profession's Diversity, Equity and Inclusion Journey

✓ Have you evaluated your employer or prospective employer's commitment to diversity?

✓ Who are your role models?

✓ Do you understand the difference between a mentor and a sponsor?

Chapter 7: Core Values that Every Accountant Should Embrace

✓ How would you grade yourself on the strength of your character?

✓ Would you be willing to do the right thing even if it negatively impacted you in the short term?

✓ Are you committed to a high standard of personal conduct?

Chapter 8: Developing and Enhancing Your Technical Skills

✓ Are you committed to continuous lifelong learning?

✓ Are you in the habit of asking thoughtful questions to facilitate learning?

✓ Are you willing to share your knowledge and experience with others?

Chapter 9: Working Effectively with Others

✓ Are you a good listener?

✓ Do you do a good job setting expectations with others?

✓ Do you follow the "Golden Rule" (i.e., treat others the way you would like to be treated)?

Chapter 10: Developing Your Communication Skills

✓ Do you double check your written communications before providing them to others?

✓ Do you prepare thoroughly before making a formal presentation?

✓ Do you ask questions to confirm that your instructions were understood?

Chapter 11: Blocking and Tackling: The Importance of Being Organized and Nailing Both Big and Small Tasks

✓ Do you "sweat the details?"

✓ Are you doing your part to support the goals of the broader organization?

✓ Are you focused on doing as good a job as you can in your current role as opposed to thinking about what is next for you?

Chapter 12: Have a Value-Creation Mindset

✓ Do you routinely solicit feedback from those you work with?

✓ What suggestions can you offer to improve the current state at your employer?

Chapter 13: Embrace Change—Technology Is Your Friend!

✓ Are you investing in your technology skills?

✓ Do you make it a point to get out in front of a "change cycle"?

✓ Do you believe that change creates opportunity?

Chapter 14: Relationships, Relationships, Relationships

✓ Do you think broadly about relationship possibilities?

✓ Have you stayed in touch with your classmates?

✓ Do you follow up the next day after meeting a new contact?

Chapter 15: Character Traits that Can Help You Succeed

✓ Do you focus on things that are within your control as opposed to worrying about things you cannot control?

✓ How well do you handle adversity?

✓ Are you a team player?

Chapter 16: How to Avoid Burnout

✓ Does your work provide you with sufficient challenges?

✓ Do you proactively manage your work and home life to avoid burnout?

✓ Are you taking care of yourself?

Chapter 17: Career Transitions: How to Make Good Decisions

✓ Have you had candid conversations with your current employer about any concerns you may have about your present position, including letting them know that you are considering resigning?

✓ Have you objectively considered the "pros and cons" of leaving versus staying?

✓ Have you thought about the longer-term implications of your decision?

Chapter 18: The Importance of Giving Back

✓ How many people are you coaching or mentoring?

✓ Have you thanked the people who contributed to your success lately?

Some Concluding Words of Advice and Encouragement: Always set your standards high! Think positively and set aggressive goals. Believe in yourself and you will be amazed at what you accomplish!

 Final Food for Thought

The quality of a person's life is in direct proportion to their commitment to excellence, regardless of their chosen field of endeavor.

—Vince Lombardi, NFL Coach, whose Green Bay Packers won the first and second Super Bowls (the National Football League's Super Bowl trophy is named in his honor)

Acknowledgments

This book would not have been possible without the support and assistance of many individuals and I would be remiss if I did not formally acknowledge and thank them for their help.

A number of current or recently graduated college accounting students made the time to read all or portions of my draft manuscript and offer valuable suggestions and feedback. Thank you to John Garavento, Vince Mallet, Deandra Turchi, John Villarante, Brianna Vechesky, Nathan Vrabel and Billy Sikora! You shared some great insights from the vantage point of a student or early-career professional that helped improve this book.

A professional colleague of mine, Dean Junkans, who has written several books himself, offered helpful advice in the early stages of the project regarding the organization and layout of the book. Likewise, my brother Kevin looked at an early draft and provided some excellent suggestions, including one that became the inspiration for Chapter Six.

A few of my former KPMG colleagues similarly offered helpful editorial and organizational suggestions, so thank you Frank Ross, Bill McKeown and Bette Kozlowski.

My friends at the Pennsylvania Institute of Certified Public Accountants also aided my efforts. Thank you to their CEO, Mike Colgan, as well as my fellow PICPA (CPA Journal) Editorial Board members Dave Wagaman and Michael Zaydon, each of whom made the time to review a draft of the document and provide helpful feedback. Maureen Renzi, a retired PICPA Communications professional, also shared some valuable feedback at a key juncture in my drafting process.

Another good friend of mine, Tom Foley, offered several great tips and shared his wisdom regarding my use of quotations. His advice improved this book. And Dr. Stephanie Weidman, who leads the accounting program at Rowan University, offered some valuable suggestions throughout but specifically related to the "Afterword."

Jeanette Franzel, CPA, who had a distinguished career in public service with the federal Government Accountability Office (GAO) and subsequently as a board member of the Public Company Accounting Oversight Board (PCAOB), graciously made the time to read my manuscript and provided very detailed comments, observations and feedback. Her insights were invaluable. I have incorporated virtually all of her suggestions into the final version of the document and am confident the value of this book to students and professionals of all ages has been enhanced by her contributions.

John Nickolas, Larry McAlee and Ed Hanway, a few very successful CPAs and good friends, kindly reviewed a draft of my manuscript and provided testimonials on the book. Thanks guys, for your help.

Just when I thought I was about finished, I was introduced to a terrific editor and seasoned professional writer, Craig Stock, who graciously "fixed" all the grammatical, structural and other flaws that this first-time author had missed. Craig offered other valuable advice that helped me get this book to the finish line. I also need to thank my pal Jack Brennan for introducing me to Craig. Much appreciated! Jack also made the time to review the book and provide some great feedback and a helpful introduction.

I also had the benefit of having one of the best graphic arts professionals I have ever worked with assist me with the design and layout of the book. Rob Cuff, you are an extremely talented individual and I very much appreciated your creative approach to making this book better (and definitely more fun)!

Thanks also to Bill Falloon, Samantha Enders, Purvi Patel and their colleagues at Wiley as they professionally managed the editing and production process and patiently answered my many questions about the world of book publishing.

Finally, I am thankful that my former colleague on the AICPA Foundation Board, Ernie Almonte, wrote a very gracious introduction to the book. Ernie, if I ever run for office, I am hiring you as my campaign manager! With appreciation to all.

—Jerry Maginnis

About the Author

We are all products of our backgrounds and experiences. This book was based on mine. I'm providing this brief summary of my career path to offer perspective and context as to how the opinions and views expressed in this book were shaped.

I spent virtually my whole career in public accounting. I am a CPA and an auditor by background and training. Early in my career, I had the opportunity to work with many types of clients in a variety of industries. I served publicly and privately held companies, large and small. I also worked with clients in the nonprofit and governmental sectors. As an audit partner, I specialized in serving emerging growth companies. Many of them were venture capital backed and eventually went public. This taught me a lot about capital formation in our economy. My clients were also active in merger and acquisition transactions, which gave me insights about business combinations and how they can benefit investors and other stakeholders.

In 2002, I was asked to become the leader of KPMG's audit practice in Pennsylvania, overseeing about 40 audit partners and about 400 professionals in our Philadelphia, Harrisburg and Pittsburgh offices. In this role, I was responsible for the top-line growth and bottom-line profitability of the practice, as well as managing the people, including headcount and compensation decisions. I was also ultimately responsible for the quality of our work and our clients' satisfaction with our service.

In 2006, I became the Philadelphia Office Managing Partner (OMP) for the Firm. As OMP, I had responsibility for all three of the firm's major businesses: audit, tax, and advisory. It was my job to build a strong culture, one in which our employees felt that the firm was a great place to work and to advance their careers. As managing partner, I spent a lot of time with our clients and employees and representing KPMG in the Philadelphia business community. I was a member of the board and the executive committee of the Greater Philadelphia Chamber of Commerce and served on the CEO Council for Growth, an organization focused on economic development and business expansion in the Philadelphia region.

In 2014–2015, I served as president of the Pennsylvania Institute of CPAs (PICPA). During my tenure, the PICPA, one of 50 state CPA societies, had about 22,000 members, making it the nation's fourth-largest state CPA society. While the PICPA had many members from the Big Four and other large accounting firms, much of its membership comprised CPAs working in industry and from regional and local firms (and even sole practitioners). Serving in this role afforded me extensive contact with CPAs from firms and organizations of all sizes and enhanced my awareness of their challenges and opportunities.

During the year I served as PICPA president, I was a designated representative on the Council of the AICPA, followed by a three-year term as a member of the Council. AICPA Council meets each spring and fall to hear updates from the organization's leadership and to address issues facing the profession. Guest speakers at its three-day meetings included members of Congress and corporate CEOs. The meetings were always an interesting learning experience and enabled me to expand my relationships with other CPAs from around the United States, which was valuable in many ways, including broadening my perspective on a variety of topics.

Upon retiring from KPMG on September 30, 2015, I joined the board of the Cohen & Steers mutual fund complex. I serve as chairman of the audit committee for these funds. More recently, I joined the board of inTEST Corporation, a publicly traded technology company listed on the New York Stock Exchange. I serve as the chair of the board's audit committee. I am also serving as a Senior Advisor, Strategy and Growth, to the CEO and management team of Centri Business Consulting, LLC. Centri is a firm that specializes in providing financial reporting, internal controls, valuation, technical accounting research and CFO advisory services to their clients

In 2016, I became "Executive in Residence" for the accounting program at Rowan University in Glassboro, N.J. Rowan has about 500 accounting majors from diverse backgrounds. Many students have transferred to Rowan after completing a two-year community college program. My role entails providing the students with guest lectures on such topics as ethics, careers in accounting and current developments in accounting and auditing. I also arrange for guest speakers from the profession to come to campus to speak to our students. I endeavor to be a resource to students as they contemplate their transition from academia into the workforce and have met with many of them for informal coaching and mentoring sessions. I also have served as the chair of the University's Accounting Advisory Board and a moderator for its Beta Alpha Psi chapter. In connection with my involvement at Rowan, I have become a member of the American Accounting Association, the largest community of accountants in academia, who shape the future of accounting through teaching and research.

I am a past board member of the AICPA Foundation, where I served as treasurer, and the PICPA Foundation, where I served as chairman. Both institutions focus on grooming and creating opportunities for the next generation of CPAs. Both organizations also have strategic ties to college and university accounting programs and are working to create a more diverse profession. These ties made for good synergies with my role and work at Rowan.

So, in summary, this book is based not only on what I have learned in my 40-plus years as a practicing CPA, but on experiences in academia, my exposure to state CPA societies, the AAA and the AICPA, and my continuing involvement in the business world. These varied experiences have provided exposure to just about all aspects of the accounting profession, and in the preceding pages I have attempted to share things I've learned that might be helpful to students, early-career professionals, and accountants of all ages.

About the Website

During the preparation of the book, one of the reviewers suggested to me that the "50 questions" section at the end of the book would be a helpful resource as a laminated card that could be used as a bookmark. If readers would like to create their own version of such a card, we are making this section available as a resource that can be downloaded by visiting:

www.wiley.com\go\maginnis\adviceforasuccessfulcareer
    (Password: Maginnis123)

50 Questions Card (Questions to Consider While Reading)

Index